SECRETS & LIES
MILITARY
INTELLIGENCE

SECRETS & LIES
MILITARY INTELLIGENCE

EXPOSING THE TRUTH BEHIND HISTORY'S DEADLIEST OPERATIONS

JEREMY HARWOOD

APPLE

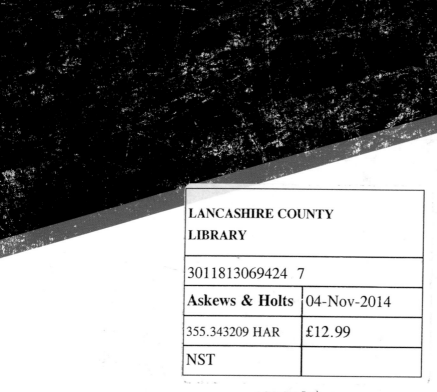
A Quantum Book

First published in the UK in 2014 by
Apple Press
74-77 White Lion Street
London N1 9PF
United Kingdom

www.apple-press.com

ISBN: 978-1-84543-590-5
QTM.SLMI

This book was conceived, designed, and produced by
Quantum Publishing Limited
6 Blundell Street
London N7 9BH
United Kingdom

Publisher: Sarah Bloxham
Quantum Editorial: Sam Kennedy and Hazel Eriksson
Production Manager: Rohana Yusof
Design: Amazing 15

Manufactured in China by 1010 Printing International Ltd.

10 9 8 7 6 5 4 3 2 1

Contents

Introduction

IN SOME FORM or other, military intelligence has been around for almost as long as organized warfare itself. More than 2,000 years ago, for instance, Sun Tzu, a Chinese Taoist thinker, produced a short, but immensely influential book, called succinctly *The Art of War*. Its final chapter was entitled 'On the Use of Spies'.

Sun began with what he obviously intended as a defining statement. 'What enables an intelligent government and a wise military leadership to overcome others and achieve extraordinary accomplishments', he wrote, 'is foreknowledge'. This, Sun postulated, 'cannot be got from ghosts and spirits, cannot be had by analogy and cannot be found out by calculation. It must be found out from people – people who know the conditions of the enemy.' He went on to define five different varieties of spy – what he termed local spies, inward spies, converted spies, doomed spies and surviving spies. He also discussed the various channels through which a commander could discover the strength, position and intentions of his enemies.

Before Sun's time, during it, and for centuries afterwards, the collection and transmission of military intelligence was almost exclusively by word of mouth. Scouting parties reported verbally to their commanders, prisoners answered their interrogators and diplomats personally passed on what they had learned about foreign territories. Half a world away, the Romans were putting such practices to good use. Diplomats, traders, messengers, clients and spies became Rome's eyes and ears as its imperial expansion began, particularly in the Near and Middle East.

The Romans, of course, were not the only people to make use of spies in Classical times. The Babylonians and Assyrians were certainly employing them by the 2nd millennium BC. So, too, were the Persians – both Herodotus and Xenophon described their spy system with unconcealed admiration. As for the Carthaginians, they had long been experts in intelligence-gathering before the Punic Wars brought them into a life-or-death confrontation with their Roman foes.

Hannibal, in particular, made brilliant use of the intelligence his spies provided when he took on the might of Rome during the Second Punic War. Through his spies in Rome, he learned, for instance, that the Romans were planning a two-pronged attack on Carthage's capital and the Carthaginian Spanish Empire. The Roman plan was to transport legions by sea via Massilia (modern-day Marseilles) to invade Carthage's Spanish territories south of the River Ebro, while a second army was sent south to North Africa to strike directly at Carthage itself. To prevent the implementation of the Roman plan, Hannibal decided to invade Italy and strike at Rome itself. The Carthaginian intelligence network abetted Hannibal's crossing of the Alps. His spies had already reconnoitred the terrain over which the Carthaginians would have to pass, establishing contact with friendly tribes who would be willing to provide the Carthaginians with troops, supplies and guides. Intelligence turned what on the surface appeared a risky political and military gamble into something no more perilous than any other course of action.

What this goes to show is that, contrary to what previous generations of intelligence historians claimed, the story of military intelligence goes back much further in time than the Renaissance, which they took as its starting point. It also demonstrates how, even in what might be described as more primitive times, intelligence systems were instrumental in shaping the policies of nations in both war and peace.

Spies themselves have been much the same across the ages as well. Nor have the motives of traitors changed that much over the same timescale. Some spies, like the young 18th-century American Nathan Hale, were out-and-out patriots. There is no doubt that, when Hale told his executioners just before he was hanged that he could 'only regret that I have but one life to lose for my country', he meant every word he said.

The case of the English nurse Edith Cavell is as compelling. After Brussels was captured and occupied by the Germans in August 1914, the first month of World War 1, Cavell chose to remain at her post at the Berkendael Institute. In August 1915, German authorities arrested her and accused her of helping

British and French prisoners-of-war, as well as Belgians hoping to serve with the Allied armies, to escape Belgium for neutral Holland.

During her subsequent court-martial, Cavell admitted that she was guilty of the offences with which she had been charged. She was sentenced to death. Though US and Spanish diplomats tried to get the sentence commuted, their efforts were ultimately in vain. The night before her execution on 12 October, Cavell told Reverend Horace Graham, a chaplain from the American Legation: '... this I would say, standing as I do in view of God and eternity: I realize that patriotism is not enough.'

The noble motives inspiring Cavell's undercover activities throw those of others into sharp focus. In the case of Aldrich Ames, a KGB mole inside the CIA for nine years until his eventual discovery, it was simply greed. He was in the spying game for the money. As a reward for his treachery, the KGB paid him more than $2 million; it kept another $2 million earmarked for him in a Moscow bank account. Undoubtedly Ames holds the record as the highest-paid spy in the world.

In other documented instances, the motivation appears to be more ambivalent. Colonel Alfred Redl was a classic case in point. The question is, was he blackmailed or simply bribed?

Outwardly, Redl was one of the rising stars of the Austro-Hungarian General Staff, who had become his country's top spy-catcher prior to World War I. In fact, he was a closet homosexual, who had been selling Austria-Hungary's most closely-guarded military secrets to the Russians for years. In 1911, he had arranged for Austria-Hungary to swap intelligence information with Germany. Two years later, the Germans alerted their Austrian counterparts to a suspicious envelope posted from Berlin, addressed to Nikon Nizetas, c/o General Delivery, Vienna. The Germans had opened the envelope and found that it contained 6,000 Austrian kroner and the addresses of two houses – one in Paris and one in Geneva – both known hideouts for Russian spies.

The Germans re-sealed the envelope and sent it on to Vienna's General Post Office, where two Austrian detectives were assigned to stake out the premises. For six weeks, nothing happened and when the bell finally rang, the detectives were caught off-guard. They dashed to the post office only to find that their quarry had just left. They bolted into the street after him, barely in time to catch a glimpse of a departing cab. One of them jotted down the number of the licence plate.

In an effort to salvage something from the slip-up, the detectives questioned the postal clerk, hoping to at least get a description of the suspect. But the clerk could tell them only that Nizetas had been a well-dressed man of medium height who had kept a grey hat pulled down over his face. Stumped, the two detectives shuffled back to the street, where they had an extraordinary stroke of luck. The cab that had eluded them ten minutes earlier had returned. The driver told them he had taken his fare to the Hotel Klomser.

At the hotel, the detectives asked the concierge if a certain Nikon Nizetas was among the guests. When the concierge shook his head, they asked if a man in a grey hat had arrived within the last half hour. He told them it was Redl. The detectives could scarcely believe their ears. Could Redl possibly be Nizetas? The detectives, however, had been gifted another stroke of luck. The mysterious Nizetas had left the sheath to a pen knife in the cab, evidently after using the knife to open his envelopes. The detectives gave the sheath to the concierge with instructions to ask Redl if he had lost it when he came downstairs. Two hours later, a smartly uniformed Redl descended the staircase to the lobby as the two detectives hid themselves behind a potted plant. 'Pardon me, Colonel Redl', enquired the concierge, 'but did you possibly misplace this knife sheath?' 'Why yes', said Redl, absent-mindedly. Then he froze, suddenly realizing that he had betrayed himself.

Just after midnight, four grim-faced army officers knocked at the door of Redl's room. One handed him a revolver. The decision to force him to commit suicide had been taken by Field Marshal Conrad von Hötzendorf, chief of the Imperial General Staff. No one knew better how devastating it would be to the army's reputation if Redl were to be publically exposed as a Russian spy.

It will never be known for certain whether the Russians used Redl's homosexuality to blackmail him into spying for them, or whether he sold secrets willingly to finance his undercover lifestyle. Whatever the truth, he helped bring about the deaths of hundreds of thousands of his compatriots and may well have been the greatest traitor in history.

Something powerful must have been Redl's motivating force, as is the case for all those willing to accept the strains and dangers of life undercover. Spies are undoubtedly a race apart – brave, ruthless and indispensable to the countries they serve, and the scourge of those they betray.

Their exploits unfailingly amaze and excite us. These are just tasters for what follows. Read on and enjoy!

Frumentarii

The Emperor's eyes and ears who kept watch over a mighty Empire, the frumentarii were the world's first professional intelligence service

IN A QUIET corner of a *taberna* in Roman London, some 1,950 years ago, a cloaked man nibbled at his olives and dried figs, and took occasional sips of *posca* – a mixture of water and sour wine. Partially masked by the smoke from guttering oil lamps, he went almost unnoticed by the men sitting round the cooking braziers. But he heard and noted everything that they said. Within months, information about the mood of the people, local scandals or even a rebellion in the planning had made its way back to Rome.

It is a long way from our world of instant communications, computers, bugging and hacking. Yet this man was a *frumentarius*, a member of the world's first intelligence service – and it was highly professional, well-organized and completely ruthless.

In the days when Rome was a republic, ruled by about 900 senators of high-ranking family, a secret service could not have existed. There was no bureaucracy in place to control it, and with so many rival factions in the Senate, no senators would have

FACT FILE

CREATED: Some time before AD 100

MISSION: To keep the emperor informed about political and military plots and scandals and to assassinate or otherwise neutralize his enemies

INTELLIGENCE TECHNIQUES: Led by the Princeps Peregrinorum, a senior centurion who reported directly to the emperor and the Praetorium (the legions' general staff), around 200 *frumentarii* operated throughout the empire, supported by *delatores* (informers) and *speculatores* (messengers); each legion had 5–10 frumentarii attached to it

FATE: Disbanded by Emperor Diocletian *c.* AD 300 after an outcry against their corruption and cruelty; superseded by *agentes de rebus* (general agents)

felt safe with spies around them. The legions needed intelligence, though, as they set out to conquer more and more of the known world, and the Senate needed information about what was going on in these distant lands. It was provided by the *speculatores* (scouts) about ten of whom are thought to have been appointed to each legion. They were also couriers – between the legions and provincial governors, and between the governors and the Senate in Rome – and, when necessary, clandestine executioners.

After Augustus had made himself emperor in 27 BC and cut the number of senators by a third, it had become clear that a more organized, centrally controlled body was needed to help govern Rome's growing Empire and to look after the Emperor's personal interests. At first, this was a network of *declatores* (informers) who reported to the Praetorian Guard, the Emperor's elite bodyguard in Rome. However, this system was far from effective, as Domitian realized when he took the imperial purple in AD 81; three of the eight previous emperors were known to have been murdered (two of them with the help of the Praetorian Guard) and another three were also thought to have been killed, probably by poison.

Above: The emperor Domitian who founded the Frumentarii to help him suppress corruption and spy on those he suspected of religious impropriety. However, they could not save him from assassination.

Domitian, having a healthy regard for his own skin, decided to improve his chances of survival.. He turned to the supply section of the Praetorium (the legions' general staff) and the men who provided supplies for the legions throughout the Empire: the *frumentarii* (*frumentum* means 'grain'). They were ideal for his purposes, because as well as being trained soldiers they were usually junior officers known as *principales,* and often even held the rank of centurion. The nature of their job demanded a detailed knowledge of the

Above: Hadrian (left) was emperor from AD 117 to AD 138. Vibia Sabina (right), his wife, was denounced by the frumentarii for her affair with Suetonius, the noted historian and Hadrian's secretary.

provinces in which they worked, as they hunted down grain and supplies of every type wherever they were. Such men could easily blend in with the military administration, making the fact that they were spies far less obvious.

In order to make sure that the new frumentarii were not aligned to any faction within the Senate or Imperial Court, Domitian conscripted frumentarii from every province and based them in a spies' headquarters in the Castra Peregrinorum (*peregrinorum* means 'of the foreigners') on the Caelian Hill, one of Rome's famous seven hills. There they reported to their senior centurion, the Princeps Peregrinorum, who, in turn, reported directly to the Emperor, or, in his place, to the Praetorian Guard. Significantly, they remained attached to their original legion throughout their service, whether in Rome or not, so that they did not have other allegiances in the capital. They were proud of this fact, as several tombstone inscriptions testify.

From the Castra Peregrinorum, frumentarii travelled the *Cursus Publicus* (the network of state highways that criss-crossed the Empire, first established by Augustus and ever-growing) returning to their provinces to become

Domitian's eyes, ears and, sometimes, secret assassins. They did so in style, because they had the right to stay in official residences en route and requisition anything they pleased. And by the same network they sent regular *notaria* ('written reports') back to the Emperor in Rome, full of information gleaned themselves and by the declatores about what was going on behind the scenes in each province.

Domitian's concept was good in theory, but only partly successful in practice. Ironically, after ruling for 15 years he was murdered by court officials in AD 96.

Yet the frumentarii must have become better at their job, because the next seven emperors all died of natural causes. One of them, Hadrian, who took the purple in AD 117, realized that he needed to keep a closer eye on the Senate and Imperial Court. He also sought to increase levels of surveillance on provincial generals (three previous emperors – Galba, Vitellus and Vespasian – had been put in power by legions in the provinces), as well as potentially subversive characters such as senators and even early Christians.

Under Hadrian, the frumentarii became notorious for knowing everybody's secrets – and for telling them to the Emperor. The *Historia Augusta*, a late-Roman collection of biographies of the emperors, gives us two examples. In the first, Hadrian is told in AD 119, while away from Rome, that his wife, Vibia

FRUMENTARII IN ACTION

THERE ARE VERY few accounts of how the *frumentarii* worked, because, obviously, their organization was essentially secret and existed some 1,750 years ago. But a story told by the historian Herodian of Antioch, written in the early third century AD, shows how cunning and ruthless they could be.

When Rome's Senate turned against the Emperor Maximinus Thrax in AD 238, it favoured a father and son, both named Gordian, who were invested with the imperial purple during a revolt in Africa. But both Emperor Gordians died in Africa, leaving the Senate to rue its decision - especially because Maximinus was notorious for his savagery and barbarism. The frumentarii, by now loyal to Balbinus and Pupienus, the Senate's new appointees as joint emperors, were called in and asked to dispose of Vitalius, the Prefect of the Praetorian Guard and a close ally of Maximinus.

The frumentarii, purporting to come from Maximinus, visited Vitalius with an urgent letter - some accounts say that it was folded in a distinctive way; others that it was sealed with what appeared to be his ring. The ruse gave them admittance, and Vitalianus was told that there was further information that could only be given in secret. Then in a private room, they cut him down. Having persuaded the soldiers guarding him that Maximinus himself had ordered the killing - easy to believe, because the life of a high official in Rome was often short and always perilous - they escaped.

In due course, Maximinus was assassinated, too - but whether by the frumentarii is not known.

Above: The reliefs on Trajan's Column, a landmark of imperial Rome, show scenes from his Dacian campaigns (AD 101–102 and AD 105–106). Trajan relied on special scouts called *exploratores* for military intelligence behind enemy lines.

Sabina, is having an affair with his secretary, the noted historian Suetonius Tranquillis, the author of *de Vita Caesarum* (*The Life of the Caesars*/*The Twelve Caesars*) and *de Viris Illustribus* (*On Illustrious Men*). The accusation may have been true, because Vibia Sabina is known to have had an unconventional view of marriage and had married at an early age; Hadrian, too, was notorious for having affairs with married women. At any rate, Hadrian fired the eminent Suetonius immediately – or, rather, he tasked the frumentarii with doing so – and, he said 'would have sent away his wife too, on the ground of temper and irritability, had he been merely a private citizen'. Later, many others were 'sent away', because 'without his consent they had been conducting themselves towards his wife ... in a more informal way than the etiquette of the court demanded'.

Presumably Hadrian was reconciled with Vibia Sabina, making allowances for her temper and irritability, though he himself, after building his famous 80-mile long wall across Britain, took a Greek youth, Antinous, as a lover – and made the boy a god after he drowned in Egypt. On Vibia's death, in AD 136, he deified her, too. No doubt the frumentarii kept a close watch on them both.

Hadrian did not confine the efforts of his frumentarii to spying on his wife's relationships: the friends of Antinous, the plots of the Imperial Court and possible rebellions in the provinces were also surveilled, as the *Historia Augusta* tells us, in a 1921 translation. 'Moreover, his vigilance was not confined to his own household but extended to those of his friends, and by means of his private agents [the frumentarii] he even pried into all their secrets, and so skilfully that they were never aware that the Emperor was acquainted with their private lives until he revealed it himself.'

'In this connection, the insertion of an incident will not be unwelcome, showing that he found out much about his friends. The wife of a certain man wrote to her husband, complaining that he was so preoccupied by pleasures and baths that he would not return home to her, and Hadrian found this out through his private agents. And so, when the husband asked for a furlough, Hadrian reproached him with his fondness for his baths and his pleasures. Whereupon the man exclaimed: "What, did my wife write to you just what she wrote to me?"'

Over the next 200 years after the death of Hadrian, in AD 138, the frumentarii came out into the open, slowly but surely, and left the secret world behind them. They wore the uniform of their associated legion on many occasions, carrying special insignia – some authorities believe that this involved a lance's head. They became more and more active, too, with what seems to have been the intention of setting up a 'police state' and to such effect that they became known as *curiosi*, or 'snoops and busybodies'. Soon, frumentarii were found running prisons, mines, quarries, public works and even entertainments, and sometimes acting as tax-collectors in the provinces.

Taken together with their corruption, brutality and authoritarianism – it was said that they behaved like a plundering army – it is hardly surprising that the frumentarii were universally hated. Eventually something had to be done, and the Emperor Diocletian (AD 285 to 305) took the matter in hand. He disbanded the frumentarii and replaced their 200-odd strength with a 1,200 strong corps of *agentes de rebus* (usually called 'general agents', though the literal translation is the wonderfully sinister and allusive phrase 'those who are active in matters') who were recruited from the civilian population. Civilians they may have been originally, but they were given military titles and privileges. It seems likely that the frumentarii managed to live on under another guise – certainly the agentes de rebus came to be hated by the Roman public just as much as the frumentarii had ever been.

Sir Francis Walsingham

The pious, tight-lipped Puritan who, as Elizabeth I's master-spy, created an underground intelligence network to expose domestic plotters and thwart his country's foreign enemies

WELL-OFF, WELL-CONNECTED, an ardent Protestant and utterly devoted to his queen, it was no surprise that Francis Walsingham was more than willing to enter Elizabeth I's service, when William Cecil, later Lord Burghley, recruited him in 1568. What was unexpected was the path his career took over the years that followed until persistent and prolonged bouts of ill-health brought about his resignation and death 22 years later. Officially, after a spell as English ambassador in Paris, Walsingham became Secretary to the Queen's Council. Behind the scenes, he acted as the Queen's undercover eyes and ears. He became Elizabethan England's first and greatest spymaster.

FACT FILE

BORN: c.1532, Scadbury Park, Chislehurst, Kent

DIED: 6 April 1590

MISSION: Between 1568 and 1590 successfully uncovered three plots to overthrow Elizabeth I; discovered the evidence that led to Mary, Queen of Scots, being condemned to death for treason; spied on the preparations for the Spanish Armada

INTELLIGENCE TECHNIQUES: Set up Europe-wide network of 'intelligencers' (spies), recruited double agents, conducted counter-espionage operations, decoded ciphers and secret writing

FATE: Died of a long-standing illness, either testicular cancer, kidney stones, urinary infection or diabetes

LEGACY: Founder of Britain's first Secret Service

The story started in August 1568, when Cecil summoned Walsingham to see him to discuss a matter that was too confidential to be committed to paper. Cecil told his visitor that he had received disturbing news from Sir Henry Norris, the English ambassador in Paris. The dispatch, partly written in cipher, warned Cecil that the Guises, the most powerful aristocratic family in France, were behind a planned Catholic uprising that, if successful, would bring about 'the alteration of religion and the advancement of the Queen of Scots to the crown'. The Spanish also became involved in the plan. Cecil, who had a healthy respect for Walsingham's quick wits and intelligence, asked him to investigate.

Walsingham agreed to undertake the task. His own enforced exile on the Continent during the reign of the fiercely Catholic Mary I had served to cement his Protestant beliefs still further. To him, it was unthinkable that another Catholic monarch should ever be propelled onto the throne to restore the old religion.

Norris had suggested a spy in Paris that the English might employ – a certain Captain Franchiotto, an Italian soldier and a Protestant. He had been in the service of the French for many years, but was now ready to defect. Walsingham, who was fluent in Italian, became, in espionage parlance, his 'handler'. Franchiotto quickly proved his worth. He produced detailed lists of possible Catholic secret agents. He warned that Elizabeth must be on her guard against attempts to poison her food and drink. He finally warned Walsingham that a number of troop ships were mustering at Marseilles, ready to carry soldiers to aid the Catholic rebels if and when they rose in the north of England. The ultimate object was to overthrow Elizabeth and place Mary, Queen of Scots, on the throne of England.

Much though Cecil and Walsingham might have disputed it, there was no denying the fact that Mary had a surprisingly strong claim to the English crown. James V of Scotland, her father, whom she succeeded at the age of six, was the son of Margaret, Henry VIII's older sister. This put Mary, as well as Elizabeth, in the direct line of descent from Henry VII – Elizabeth as his granddaughter and Mary as his great-granddaughter. As far as Catholics were concerned, Elizabeth had no claim to the throne at all. As the daughter of Anne Boleyn, she was illegitimate.

On 16 May 1568, Mary arrived in England, driven out of Scotland by her rebellious Protestant nobles who had forced her to abdicate in favour of

Previous page: In a portrait attributed to John De Critz the Elder, Sir Francis Walsingham looks every inch the ruthless spymaster.

Opposite: The 'invincible' Spanish Armada takes to the seas. Walsingham's spies alerted him to its preparation; the invaluable information they provided included the news that its sailing would be delayed for a year. This gave England the time it needed to prepare.

THE CATHOLIC WHO SPIED ON THE ARMADA

ANTONY STANDEN WAS a Roman Catholic refugee from Elizabethan England. He was also one of Walsingham's most important secret agents. The exact date when he turned spy is uncertain, but by 1587, he was being paid what was then the enormous sum of £100 per year for his services. He certainly earned his money. Operating under the pseudonym of Pompeo Pellegrini, Standen, who had settled in Italy and become a close friend of Giovanni Figliazzi, Tuscany's ambassador to Madrid, was tasked with finding out all he could about the preparations for the Spanish Armada and when it would be ready to strike.

Standen sent a Flemish man – 'a proper fellow' who 'writes well' – to Lisbon. Though he prudently never named him, he did reveal that the Fleming's brother was one of the secretaries to the Marquis de Santa Cruz, Philip II's Grand Admiral. The two Flemings obtained a list of all the ships, men and supplies earmarked for the Spanish fleet. It proved that the Armada would not be ready to sail for at least another year. Walsingham passed the intelligence to Sir Francis Drake, who used it to help plan his attack on the Spanish fleet at Cadiz. It was a huge success. Afterwards, Walsingham wrote to Standen to tell him that the queen herself was 'grateful for his work and hopes that he will continue to serve her well'.

her infant son. She had managed to escape from captivity but failed in an attempt to regain the throne by force of arms. Now she was seeking Elizabeth's help. She did not receive it. Instead, confronted by ill-concealed hostility, she was put under house arrest. Mary took what seemed like the only option left open to her. She turned to conspiracy.

The following year, the northern Catholics rose, led by Charles Neville, Earl of Westmorland and Thomas Percy, Earl of Northumberland. The revolt, however, was short-lived. Northumberland was captured and executed in York; Westmorland fled the country, eventually to join the Spanish army in the Netherlands. What Walsingham had to establish was whether or not Mary herself had been involved in the plot.

Shortly before the rising, a new character had come onto the scene. He was Roberto di Ridolfi, a Florentine banker who was highly respected in the City of London. He even acted as a financial agent for Cecil himself. What no one suspected was that, since 1566, he had been a clandestine agent for Pope Pius V, who put him in charge of handling the money he had earmarked to fund the Catholic cause in England.

From the Pope's point of view, Ridolfi was ideally qualified for the job. His profession gave him the ability to move freely around the courts of Europe. His banking contacts in Florence helped him to shift funds through bills of exchange rather than having to arrange for the surreptitious transport of large amounts of cash. All went smoothly until, in September 1569, Ridolfi slipped up. On behalf of Don Guerau de Spes, the newly-appointed Spanish Ambassador, he arranged the transfer of what was then the enormous sum of £3,000 to the Bishop of Ross. The latter was Mary's representative in London.

The sheer size of the transaction made it impossible to conceal. Ridolfi was detained and taken to Walsingham's home for questioning. What exactly transpired after his arrest is far from certain, but there is little doubt that he offered to collaborate with his captors. Elizabeth herself got in on the act. Observing that some of Ridolfi's disclosures were 'far other than the truth is', she authorized a bargain. Ridolfi was offered clemency in exchange for a full disclosure of his dealings with Mary, Queen of Scots. Just a month later, he was freed on bail.

While no one knows for sure, it seems likely that during his captivity Walsingham persuaded Ridolfi to become a double agent. Certainly he told Cecil

Opposite: Elizabeth I is portrayed here in all her finery. It was not for nothing that she was christened Gloriana.

that he was confident that Ridolfi 'would deal both discretely and uprightly, as one both wise and who standeth on terms of honesty and reputation'.

After being granted his freedom, Ridolfi apparently resumed the task with which he had been entrusted. In March 1571, he made his way to Rome, where he presented Pius with a plan for another Catholic uprising – this time led by Thomas Howard, Duke of Norfolk. Supported by Spanish troops, the rebels would put Mary on the English throne.

The Pope endorsed the plan. Almost immediately, however, it started to unravel, either by accident or design. Charles Bailly, the Bishop of Ross's undercover courier, was arrested on his landing in Dover. Norfolk was charged with high treason, found guilty and executed on Tower Green the following year. Though Parliament bayed for Mary's blood, Mary survived, thanks to Elizabeth's decision to spare her. As for Ridolfi, he slipped back to Florence, where he entered the service of the Medici, became a Senator, and died many years later.

By this time, Walsingham was in Paris, having been sent there to take over from Norris as ambassador. He arrived in the French capital during a lull in the Wars of Religion between the Catholic and Huguenot factions that had been tearing the country apart.

The lull was not to last. In August 1572, Walsingham personally witnessed the St Bartholomew's Day Massacre, in which 2,000 Protestants were slaughtered in Paris alone. The atrocity served to strengthen his anti-Catholic sentiments even further. He told the Privy Council that the Huguenots had been attacked 'without pity and compassion, without regard for either age or sex, without ordinary form of justice'. He appealed to Elizabeth to be allowed to return home. In April 1573, Walsingham's wish was granted.

On his return to England, Walsingham doubled and redoubled his intelligence efforts. His network of agents now stretched far into Europe. At home, his surveillance concentrated more and more on the Queen of Scots and the seemingly constant swirl of plots that seemed to revolve around her person.

Walsingham was clear about what needed to be done. 'So as long as that devilish woman liveth', he raged, 'neither her majesty may make account to continue her quiet possession of her crown, nor do her faithful servants assure themselves of safety of their lives'. What Walsingham probably had in mind was Edmund Mather's plot to assassinate Cecil on his way back from court and rescue the Catholic Earl of Northumberland from imprisonment. Unfortunately for Mather, he had confided the details of the scheme to William Herle, who was one of Walsingham's undercover agents. Under interrogation, Mather was forced to confess his admiration for Mary. Had his plan succeeded, his next target would have been Elizabeth herself.

The Queen could not be persuaded, however. All that Walsingham could do was to tighten the net he was weaving around Mary. It took another 15 years for him and his spies to gather sufficient evidence to bring Mary to trial. Piece by piece, the fateful jigsaw was put together, starting with the Throckmorton plot of 1583.

Above: Philip II of Spain said it was time to put England 'to the torch' when he ordered the despatch of the Armada.

On the face of it, Francis Throckmorton was an unlikely conspirator. His father, Sir John, though a Catholic, had been vice-president of the council entrusted with the governance of the Welsh marches and had been knighted by Elizabeth for his services. Around Christmas 1581, however, the young Francis was recruited by Claude de Courcelles, an official in the French embassy in London, to handle the secret enciphered correspondence between Mary and her French supporters. His house at Paul's Wharf became a centre of intrigue.

Throckmorton survived until 1583, when Laurent Feron, a London-born clerk in the embassy, turned double agent and secretly supplied Walsingham with copies of the correspondence in the French diplomatic

bag. A Watergate-style raid on the French ambassador's secret files provided even more information. By November, Walsingham had all that he needed in order to strike.

When Walsingham's men forced their way into Throckmorton's home, they caught him in the middle of writing a letter to the Queen of Scots. That was not all they found. Further incriminating evidence included lists of safe harbours 'for landing of foreign forces', and the names of Catholic aristocrats who could be relied on to support an invasion. Throckmorton's guilt was plain. Taken to the Tower of London, where he was 'somewhat pinched' upon the rack, he revealed the full details of his conspiracy. An uprising of the Catholic nobility was to be timed to coincide with the arrival of an invasion force commanded by the Duc de Guise and bankrolled by Philip II of Spain; Throckmorton had also been intriguing with Don Bernadino de Mendoza, the Spanish ambassador. After a quick trial, he was executed the following year.

Walsingham had been predicting the launching of some enterprise of this kind for years, but the scale of Throckmorton's plot was greater than even he had expected.

If Throckmorton had been an unlikely conspirator, Anthony Babington was a muddle-headed one. His story started in 1580, when, while visiting Paris, he was persuaded to enter the Queen of Scots' service. On his return to London a year or so later, he was told that his task was to mastermind Elizabeth's assassination. He slowly began to sound out other potential conspirators.

Of these, John Ballard, a renegade Catholic priest, was probably the most fanatical. Another, John Savage, an English exile, had sworn an oath to personally kill the queen. More conspirators – 14 in all – were subsequently recruited. Among them was Robert Poley, who, Babington believed, was a Catholic spy serving in Walsingham's own household. In fact, he was an agent provocateur who was Walsingham's man from the start.

Unravelling the conspiracy depended on the successful decipherment of secret letters sent by Mary to her supporters and their replies. Gilbert Clifford, one of Walsingham's double agents, had persuaded the Queen of Scots that he had devised a foolproof means of smuggling letters in and out of her place of captivity. This involved putting them into a watertight container slim enough to slip through the bunghole of a barrel of beer.

Opposite: Mary, Queen of Scots, is led to her death in the Great Hall of Fotheringhay Castle on 8 February 1587. Like all the other great officers of state, Walsingham stayed away from her execution.

Mary's servants retrieved the inward-bound correspondence; Clifford recovered her replies from the beer's Derbyshire-based brewer, who was in his pay. As a result Walsingham was able to read Mary's correspondence before she could get her hands on it and almost as soon as her replies had been despatched.

Mary fell in eagerly with Clifford's scheme. Little did she know that not only were her letters being intercepted, but they were also being deciphered by Thomas Phelippes, another of Walsingham's 'intelligencers', who quickly broke the code Mary herself had devised. The great spymaster, however, was in no hurry to act. He was content to let the evidence against the Scottish Queen accumulate until he secured the one vital piece of information he needed. He secured this in summer 1586. The letter Mary wrote to Babington on July 18 proved she was fully involved with his plot.

Walsingham acted swiftly. Babington fled to avoid arrest, but, after ten days on the run, he was caught disguised as a farm labourer in Harrow. He and the 13 other plotters were soon standing trial for their lives. Found guilty of high treason, they were hanged, drawn and quartered on 20 September. As for Mary, she, too, faced her judges on 14 October, when a royal commission, headed by Cecil himself, arrived at Fotheringhay Castle to try her.

The queen put up a spirited defence. She started by refusing to recognize the authority of the court, saying that they lacked the competence to put a sovereign on trial. Then she launched into a vehement personal attack on Walsingham himself. 'Spies are men of doubtful credit,' she said, 'who make a show of one thing and speak another.' It was no use. Try though she might, Mary was overwhelmed by the weight of evidence against her. The commission found her guilty of high treason and sentenced her to death.

After months of prevarication, Elizabeth was persuaded to sign the warrant for her execution on 1 February 1587. It took place eight days later in the Great Hall at Fotheringhay – but did not go according to plan. The understandably nervous executioner botched the job. It took three blows of his axe to sever her head. The horrified onlookers said that, for 15 minutes afterwards, Mary's lips continued to move in silent prayer.

It was, however, Walsingham's finest hour. He and Leicester now urged Elizabeth to strike directly at the Spanish before they could attack her. Convinced by Walsingham's intelligence reports from Portugal and Spain, Elizabeth fell in with their urgings. She authorized Sir Francis Drake 'to impeach the joining together of the King of Spain's fleet.' The successful raid on Cadiz was the result. It won the time the English needed to prepare. When the Armada eventually sailed, it was defeated and dispersed.

By this time, Walsingham was mortally ill. In August 1589, he was bedridden and on 12 December he dictated and signed his will. Nevertheless, he struggled on, attending meetings of the Privy Council until towards the end of March the following year. On 1 April, he suffered a stroke. Six days later, just before midnight, he died. The day after his death, the will was found 'in a secret cabinet'. He had played the spymaster to the last.

Catholic propagandists concocted lurid accounts of Walsingham's death. According to them, 'his urine came forth at his mouth and nose with so odious a stench that none could come near him'. His body, they said, had become so corrupted that it poisoned one of the pall-bearers at his funeral. The truth was that he passed away peacefully in his bed. In his will, he had asked for a simple funeral. This took place on the evening of 7 April in the north aisle of the old St Paul's cathedral. He was placed in the same grave as Sir Philip Sidney, his son-in-law. A simple epitaph in English carved on a wooden tablet read:

'In foreign countries their intents he knew, Such was his zeal to do his country good, When dangers would by enemies ensue, As well as they themselves he understood.'

Above: Sir Francis Drake, the sea-dog who 'singed the King of Spain's beard' at Cadiz, was one of Walsingham's close intimates.

Chevalier d'Eon

A battle-hardened spy for French King Louis XV, d'Eon spent his last 33 years dressed as a woman, and latterly made a living through fencing matches – in long skirts

CHARLES-GENEVIÈVE-LOUIS-Auguste-André-Thimothée d'Eon de Beaumont was born into a noble family in Tonerre, central France, in 1728. His parents had been so desperate to have a girl, one story goes, that they gave him the name 'Geneviève' and dressed him in female clothes until the age of seven. Later, however, d'Eon was to claim that he had been born a girl, but that his father had been so desperate to have a son that he raised 'Geneviève' as one; on another occasion he said that he had been forced to masquerade as a boy in order that his family could receive a legacy. Whatever the case, the stories are typical of the mysteries, deceptions and downright lies – you might even sum them up as 'tradecraft' – with which d'Eon muddied the truth throughout his whole life.

Slim, smooth-skinned and with a somewhat girlish appearance, d'Eon showed little interest in ladies during his youth and, perhaps as a result,

FACT FILE

BORN: In late 1728 in Tonerre, Burgundy, France

DIED: 21 May 1810 in London in poverty. At post-mortem examination shown to have male organs

MISSION: As part of Louis XV's 'Secret du Roi' to foment a conspiracy, ideally with Russia, to make Louis's cousin, the Prince de Conti, King of Poland; later, while a diplomat In London, to scout English beaches to prepare for a French invasion

INTELLIGENCE TECHNIQUES: Disguise as a woman, and general intrigue in Russian and London society

FATE: Forced to live as a woman in France, later to return to London to live off his skills in fencing

LEGACY: An inspiration to modern transvestite and transgender community; hero in a 24-part Japanese animated TV series

Left: The Prince de Conti was the French king's cousin and his candidate to become King of Poland; Chevalier d'Eon was deeply involved in the conspiracy.

excelled in his education. He qualified in both civil and canon law at the College Mazarin, in Paris, aged 21, and soon made himself indispensable as a secretary and administrator in Louis XV's court. He was also an accomplished fencer and became noted for his charm and wit.

Louis XV, who ruled France between 1715 and 1774, was known for a time as *le bien aimé* – 'the well-beloved'. Historians have taken a different view – Professor Jerome Blum called him 'a perpetual adolescent called

Above: Dressed as a woman in a long black gown and a white mob cap, the Chevalier d'Eon takes part in a fencing display held at Carlton House, London, in April 1787. The Prince of Wales was among the spectators.

to do a man's job' – and his people came to agree. One example of his adolescent folly was his establishment in 1745 of *Secret du Roi* (The King's Secret), a network of spies that operated throughout Europe. Its existence was a secret to the King's foreign ministers and diplomats and often followed policies that were completely in opposition to the official government line.

One such policy was Louis' plan to install his cousin the Prince de Conti on the Polish throne. Louis thought that Empress Elizabeth of Russia might be able to help, so he sent an emissary to her court in 1756. This was a Scot in French service called the Chevalier Douglas, who took d'Eon with him as his secretary. In d'Eon's papers, discovered long after his death, he claims that he travelled dressed as a woman, pretending to be

Douglas's niece, but there is no evidence to support this. We do know, however, that he would have attended Elizabeth's weekly balls, where cross-dressing was compulsory.

The mission failed in its main purpose – though, apparently, the Empress took a considerable liking to d'Eon – and he returned to life at the French court and the affairs of Secret du Roi. But he nursed a grievance that would affect the rest of his life: he claimed that he was owed 10,000 livres for his travelling expenses and that Louis had not paid him (however, the King is reported to have granted him a pension of 2,000 livres for life, equivalent to about £30,000 today). Soon afterwards, he further endeared himself to Louis XV by disregarding the King's official policy to ask the Empress Elizabeth to help mediate peace in the Seven Years War – which ocurred between 1754 and 1763, and mainly, France and Austria on one side and Britain and Prussia on the other. Under cover of *Secret du Roi*, and abetted by his friend the Empress, d'Eon foiled the French Ambassador's plans. Obviously, his machinations had to be kept secret, which gave him even more leverage with the King.

With his mission accomplished and having returned to France, d'Eon fought with some distinction in the Seven Years War, being involved in the Battle of Villinghausen in 1761, and being wounded at Ulstrup, in the

COMPULSORY CROSS-DRESSING

THE COURT OF Elizabeth Empress of Russia from 1742 to 1762 was a byword for extravagance: according to one historian it was 'arrayed in cloth of gold ... the most luxurious garments, the most expensive foods, the rarest drinks, that largest number of servants, and they applied this standard of lavishness to their dress as well'.

The 27-year-old d'Eon found himself at the centre of this extravagance while acting as Louis XV's diplomatic envoy and spy in 1755. It is likely that he found things very much to his taste – or perhaps they helped to reveal his tastes to himself. For Elizabeth held a weekly 'Metamorphoses' ball at which men had to dress as women and vice versa, by Imperial order. Most of Elizabeth's courtiers – except, presumably, d'Eon – hated the balls, fearing that they looked extremely silly but Elizabeth loved them because, according to the Russian statesman Potemkin she was 'the only woman who looked truly fine, and completely a man ... As she was tall and powerful, male attire suited her'.

The Metamorphoses balls seem to have provided d'Eon with the first opportunity to cross-dress since his childhood. According to his memoirs, he took to the practice with some gusto, travelling through Russia in a female disguise on spying missions. D'Eon's memoirs, though, are notoriously unreliable and self-serving and there is no evidence to support this.

same year. And when the war-weary Louis XV finally decided that peace – or at least the appearance of it – was desirable, in August 1762 he chose the ever-faithful d'Eon to act as secretary to the Duc de Nivernais, who was sent to London to negotiate.

The negotiations were successful, and George III, the English King – no doubt another to have been charmed – even entrusted d'Eon with the treaty to take back to Louis XV. In return, Louis awarded d'Eon the Order of Saint Louis, allowing him to use the title 'Chevalier'. But Louis still needed his help: far from genuinely wanting peace, he planned to invade England (unknown to his ministers and diplomats) and sent d'Eon back to London as a 'minister plenipotentiary', having directed him to establish the lie of the land, and especially the lie of English beaches, preparatory to a French invasion. Foolishly, perhaps – and especially so in the case of a man who already had a grievance against him – Louis put his instructions in writing.

At first, d'Eon held the fort in London, pending the arrival of the Comte de Guerchy as the new French ambassador. He took full advantage of his position, running up debts of as much as 100,000 livres on wining, dining and ingratiating himself with the cream of London society. But when de Guerchy arrived, d'Eon was relegated to the position of his secretary and de Guerchy refused to pay his debts. Furthermore, the two men hated each other: to de Guerchy, d'Eon was a strutting feckless fop who patronized him. To d'Eon, de Guerchy was a coward (during the Seven Years war, he claimed) and worse, a member of the faction at the French court headed by Madame de Pompadour, the King's mistress, that was obsessed with finding out what the Secret du Roi actually was.

Above: D'Eon, again dressed in woman's clothes, is portrayed in old age. By this time he had left France for London, where he spent much of his time staving off his numerous creditors.

Opposite: Louis XIV started off loved by his people but ended up hated by them. He quarrelled with d'Eon when he refused to pay the latter's debts, though the two were eventually reconciled.

Matters came to a head in 1764, when d'Eon complained to Louis that de Guerchy had tried to have him poisoned. De Guerchy sued for libel, lost, and was jeered by a mob of Londoners, who had rather taken d'Eon to their hearts. However, Louis had cut off d'Eon's 2,000 livre pension and now refused to pay his debts. It was time for d'Eon to play his trump card: he still had the King's signed commission to spy in preparation for an invasion of England – in direct contravention of the treaties that had just been signed. In April 1764, he published a book revealing all his diplomatic correspondence, with the exception of matters relating to the Secret du Roi. It was unheard of for a diplomat to do such a thing, and Louis took it for the warning it was. D'Eon was awarded an annuity of 12,000 livres in 1766 and continued working as a spy in London, still popular with both the mob and aristocratic society.

We know little more about d'Eon's life in London until 1774, when two things happened. First, Louis XV died and was succeeded by Louis XVI, his son, who promptly disbanded the Secret du Roi. Second, bets were laid in London about whether d'Eon was a man or a woman – he is reported to have taken his stick to the heads of some of the bookmakers. With Louis XV dead and the Secret du Roi no more, d'Eon's commission was a declining asset, but not one that Louis cared to see made public in the near future. But d'Eon was persuaded to return to France and give up the document – for a fee, of course. There was one extraordinary condition: that d'Eon should spend the rest of his days dressed as a woman. (Cynics have it that doing so also helped him avoid a duel with de Guerchy's son.)

So d'Eon returned to France and joined the court of Louis XV, where he soon made himself ridiculous – as Princess Lamballe, a confidante to Queen Marie Antoinette, reports:

'In good earnest, on the Sunday following, the Chevalier was dressed en costume, with a large hoop, very long train, sack, five rows of ruffles, an immensely high, powdered female wig, very beautiful lappets, white gloves, an elegant fan in his hand, his beard closely shaved, his neck and ears adorned with diamond rings and necklaces and assuming all the airs and graces of a fine lady!'

'But, unluckily, his anxiety was so great, the moment the Queen made her appearance, to get a sight of Her Majesty, that, on rushing before the other ladies, his wig and head-dress fell off his head; and, before they could be well replaced, he made so ridiculous a figure, by clapping them, in his confusion, hind part before, that the King, the Queen and the whole suite, could scarcely refrain from laughing aloud in the church.'

It was all too much, for all the parties. After a fortnight, d'Eon retired to his family home in Tonerre.

By 1785, d'Eon's debts in London had caught up with him and he returned there, still dressed as a woman, to try to prevent the forced sale of his extensive library. He earned a little money by giving fencing displays, clad in a long black gown and a white cap, but eventually, in 1791,

his library was sold, along with some of his swords and his jewels. He was injured in a fencing match in Southampton in 1796 and took lodgings with a widow called Mrs Cole, who had no idea that he was anything but a woman. After six months in a debtor's prison, he returned to Mrs Cole's lodgings, suffered a fall, became paralysed and eventually died, on 21 May 1810 at the age of 81. A post mortem was held the next day, and Mr Copeland, surgeon, was able to issue a certificate proving that, all along, he had been a man.

So was d'Eon the first transgender spy? The answer is that nobody knows. His own accounts of his spying activities and of his gender are often contrived, and sometimes demonstrably false, possibly because he was always in need of money and found it useful to create controversy and create a larger-than-life character in order to obtain it. But many believe that he was. The Beaumont Society, Britain's support group for transvestites and transgender people, is named after him.

Above: Tsarina Elizabeth, dressed in a guards officer's uniform and attended by a page, is captured on horseback. A powerful, free-spirited and strong-willed woman, she was in favour of sexual freedom, especially for herself.

Nathan Hale

The young American hero who gave his life spying for George Washington in the American Revolutionary War

BY THE TIME the body of the young man had stopped twitching on the end of the noose, his soul may have already departed but in that same moment an American martyr was born. Just a minute before, the spy, caught red-handed and sentenced without a trial, had stood calmly before his British captors and, with great dignity, said the immortal line, 'I only regret that I have but one life to lose for my country'.

Hale paid the ultimate price for his cause: the liberty of America. Ever since then, opinions about him have changed along with society's attitudes and its perceptions about historical truth. Was he a good man but an incompetent spy? Or was he honourable and proficient, but just terribly unlucky?

Nathan Hale was born on 6 June 1755, in Coventry, Connecticut, the sixth child of a prosperous farmer. His heritage was one of education and learning, with Harvard graduates and Yale teachers prominent in his family, and young Nathan proved himself worthy of it. He entered Yale University at the age of 14, and graduated as one of its top 13 scholars

FACT FILE

BORN: 15 April 1755, Coventry, Connecticut
DIED: 22 September 1776, New York
MISSION: On 15 September 1776, he was sent to spy on British troops in the Revolutionary War so that George Washington could plan his assault on New York
INTELLIGENCE TECHNIQUES: Minimal – Hale used his own clothes and genuine identification documents
FATE: Caught and hanged by the British without a trial
LEGACY: The mission failed but Hale became an American legend

in 1773, aged 18. Tellingly, he belonged to Linonia, the literary fraternity, where the leading issues of the day were discussed – and one of the main bones of contention was the issue of colonial America's relationship with the British Crown.

In December of 1773, a few months after Hale's graduation, the American 'Sons of Liberty' threw a large consignment of tea into Boston Harbour, Massachusetts: the 'Boston Tea Party'. Massachusetts and neighbouring Connecticut were abuzz with talk of dissension and dissatisfaction with British rule. At the time, Nathan Hale was working as a schoolmaster at the Union School, in New London, Connecticut – not just teaching boys; before his time, he believed that girls, too, should have a proper education, so he taught a class of 20 of them between 5 and 7 in the morning.

Above: Nathan Hale, a 21-year-old American patriot, is depicted disguised as a Dutch schoolteacher spying on British positions in New York as they prepare to defend the city against George Washington's army.

Above: HMS Phoenix, Roebuck, Tartar and two smaller British vessels come under fire from American shore batteries as they try to force their way along the Hudson River.

He still paid close attention to the politics of the day, and after the Battles of Lexington and Concord, in April 1775 – the first occasion upon which American militiamen had fought and ultimately seen off British regular troops – Hale joined the Connecticut Militia, with the rank of First Lieutenant. Meanwhile, the British garrison in Boston was under siege from American militiamen and one Bernard Tallmadge, a Yale contemporary and friend of Hale and a school superintendent (also a future spymaster, with his 'Culper Ring') was there as an observer.

In early July, Tallmadge wrote to his old friend Hale, who, presumably, had asked him for advice, saying: 'Was I in your happy condition, I think the more extensive service would be my choice. Our Holy Religion, the honour of our God, a glorious country and our happy constitution is what we have to defend.' Hale shook his pupils' hands, prayed with them and enlisted as a First Lieutenant in The 7th Connecticut Regiment of

George Washington's Continental Army. And to make his position even more clear, this 20-year-old stood up at a town meeting and said: 'Let us march immediately and never lay down our arms until we obtain our independence.' This is believed to have been the first time that any 'colonial' had referred to the concept of independence in public – it was one of a number of impassioned speeches he is said to have made.

In September 1775, Hale marched with his regiment to take up a position near Boston to block British reinforcements from reaching the town, though he also revisited Connecticut on a number of occasions to recruit more soldiers. In early March 1776, having been promoted to Captain, he and his regiment were part of the successful assault on Boston, and then marched south, to New York, where events took on a momentum of their own.

First, Hale took matters into his own hands and planned an attack on HMS *Phoenix*, a British frigate. On 29 August 1776, together with four soldiers and a sergeant, he carried out a night assault and captured a

THE CULPER SPY RING

MAJOR BERNARD TALLMADGE, Nathan Hale's classmate at Yale University and the man who urged him to join the 'Continental Army', learned his lesson from Hale's unfortunate fate. In 1778, George Washington asked the then Major in the 2nd Continental Light Dragoons (he was later promoted to Colonel) to set up a network of spies who would report on the British Army's troop movements, fortifications and plans in the New York area – and do their job with a level of sophistication and professionalism that Hale had, sadly, lacked.

Crucially, Tallmadge's organization comprised a series of agents, rather than depending on a single spy. Two of them were Abraham Woodhull, a farmer who used the name 'Sam Culper Sr' and Robert Townsend, a merchant who went under the name of 'Sam Culper Jr'; Tallmadge's *nom de guerre* was 'John Bolton'. Also involved were Austin Roe, a tavern keeper, and Anna Strong, a judge's wife who used the arrangement of clothes on her washing line to signal one Caleb Brewster, a whale boat owner who could transport messages. Invisible ink, dead drops, messages in newspapers and complex codes were also used.

The Culper Ring was the most successful of all spying operations during the Revolutionary War, supplying Washington with a mass of vital information. For example, it was instrumental in scuppering an attack planned by the British on the newly arrived French fleet in Newport, Rhode Island in 1780. The Ring also exposed the treachery of General Benedict Arnold, who planned to hand the fort at West Point, New York to the British, and his handler Major John André, Britain's chief spy during the War, who was duly hung. The Culper Ring continued to provide Washington with information until the end of the war, in 1783.

Above: The day Hale chose to launch his spying mission in New York was unfortunate; a major fire burnt down a quarter of the city and put the British on the alert for possible rebel infiltrators.

tender (the vessel used to service the ship), four cannons and supplies. George Washington commended his enterprise and dash and he came to the notice of a Captain Knowlton, who had been asked by Washington to set up a force of elite soldiers who were to be despatched for 'special service' wherever they were needed. Known as 'Knowlton's Rangers', they were the forerunners of all America's special forces since; indeed, the date '1776' is inscribed on the seal of the US Army's Intelligence Service to this day. Neither Knowlton nor Hale could have guessed that the former would die at the Battle of Harlem Heights, New York, on 16 September and that the latter had only less than a week more to live.

Today we think of spies as either slightly sleazy types primarily out for money, but with a little ideology built into the mix, or as devilish James Bond characters, out for adventure. These were different times. George Washington, in desperate difficulties as his army retreated from New York, complained on 6 September, 'we have not been able to obtain the least information as to the enemy's plans.' Captain Knowlton was asked to find a volunteer officer to infiltrate New York and provide the intelligence.

Knowlton put the question to his battle-hardened Rangers, who now included Hale, but nobody volunteered – after all, spying was not considered appropriate for a gentleman and the general view, expressed by one sergeant, was 'I am willing to be shot but not to be hanged.' Yet Hale said calmly, 'I will undertake it'. This was characteristic of the young man, who took the view that it was his duty as an officer, gentleman and patriot to put the good of the whole community before his own well-being, no matter the risks.

On 14 September 1776, Hale was taken by boat from Long Island to New York. He was dressed in plain clothes and passed himself off as a Dutch schoolteacher – to prove his qualifications he carried his diploma from Yale with him, written in Latin (such a document was one of the few proofs of identity in the days before passports). There were several problems with this: first, he could not speak Dutch; second, his diploma gave his real name, which might well have been known to some of the loyalists in New York, especially following his impassioned speeches of a few years earlier; third, he had a distinctive appearance with a powder burn on his face and a hairy mole beneath his ear. Some intelligence experts have described Hale as, 'a sacrificial lamb, dispatched on a mission doomed from the start'.

If this was not bad enough, the odds were further stacked against Hale. Long Island and New York were full of 'Roger's Rangers' – a loyalist force commanded by a Major Roberts Rogers that was similar in character and purpose to the Continental Army's Knowlton's Rangers. It could well be that one of these Rangers recognized Hale (though some accounts have it that Captain Samuel Hale, Nathan's cousin and a loyalist was involved) – at any rate, he was followed in New York and arrested on 21 September, as he tried to return to Long Island.

Hale's shoes were found to contain drawings of fortifications and notes in Latin. The game was obviously up and he confessed to what he had been doing immediately. Perhaps he thought that, as had often been the case, he would be treated leniently. But these were strange, tense times – made worse by the fact that a major fire had broken out in New York on the same day, burning down a quarter of the city (it flushed out 200 partisans) – and General Sir William Howe, the British commander, was in no mood for mercy. Hale was executed the next day, aged just 21.

Below: The one-room schoolhouse where Hale worked as a teacher from 1773-1774 after graduating from Yale University. That past proved invaluable cover when spying behind enemy lines.

He received no trial, and was even refused the comfort of a Bible by his notoriously brutish gaoler, Provost Marshall Captain William Cunningham. He wrote two letters, one to his brother Enoch and one to Captain Knowlton, but Cunningham tore them up. All he had left was to die well – and he did.

For a time, the conventional view of Nathan Hale was as expressed by Rob Simmons, the US Representative for Connecticut, in a lecture titled 'Nathan Hale to Osama Bin Laden', in Autumn 2003:

'The quintessential patriot ... As much as I admire Nathan Hale ... he was a failure, and America can't afford failures ... As a people we don't like liars, but as a nation we need them.'

And former CIA Chief Richard Helms has said: 'Hale is in the American pantheon not because of what he did but why he did it.'

However, there is another view. Hale was sensible to use his own name and to go undisguised, because though by doing so he might be more likely to be caught he would also, according to the custom of the times, be much less likely to be executed. He had certainly proved his capability for 'special services' work by his attack on the *Phoenix*. We also know that he used to write to his brother Enoch using ciphers. And there are a number of mysterious absences from his regiment's camp in Long Island between May and June of 1776. Some speculate that he had been away on spying missions (one letter to Enoch refers elliptically to some such enterprise), and that the only reason we do not know about them for certain is that he had not been caught.

So it could well be that Nathan Hale was both a good guy and a good spy. The necessarily secretive nature of intelligence work means that we will probably never know the whole truth.

Below: Hale was arrested while trying to reach the American lines. The sketches of fortifications the British found concealed in his shoes were enough to condemn him. He was hanged the next day.

Benedict Arnold

Though his exploits in the Revolutionary War made him a hero, Arnold eventually turned traitor and deserted to the British. He had become disillusioned with the lack of recognition he believed he had received for his services to the American cause

THE HALLOWED WALLS of the Old Cadet Chapel in the cemetery of the US Military academy at West Point, New York, are covered with plaques and medallions, commemorating brave deeds and memorable battles. However, one plaque, situated close to the altar, differs from all the others. The name that was once deeply etched on it has been deliberately obscured. The absent name is that of Benedict Arnold, once a hero of the American Revolution who turned traitor and defected to the British at the height of the war.

Arnold's mother's family was wealthy, but his drunken father squandered his wife's money and so Arnold's inheritance. The young Arnold therefore had little choice but to become apprenticed to an apothecary in New Haven, Connecticut, eventually becoming one himself. Having fought with the Connecticut militia in the French and Indian War, Britain's decision to impose the Stamp Act on its American colonies turned him into a revolutionary. He joined

FACT FILE

BORN: 14 January 1741, Norwich, Connecticut
DIED: 14 June 1801, London
MISSION: Started spying for the British in 1779 before defecting to them openly in 1780 and serving in their army until he left America for Britain in 1781. Sold vital military secrets to the British before openly taking up arms with them and leading their forces in Virginia in the field before Lord Cornwallis arrived to take over from him
INTELLIGENCE TECHNIQUES: Codes, ciphers and smuggled letters
FATE: Compelled to live in exile for the remaining 20 years of his life
LEGACY: In US history, his name is synonymous with treachery and treason

the Sons of Liberty prior to the outbreak of the Revolutionary War.

When open conflict with Britain came, Arnold re-enlisted in his old militia, being elected to the rank of Captain by the volunteers with whom he served. His bravery in action confirmed his military ability and his devotion to the struggle for independence. He fought at the battles of Lexington and Concord and helped to attack and capture Fort Ticonderoga in upstate New York. His military career reached its apogee during the battle of Saratoga, which he planned so brilliantly that one of his contemporaries declared him to be 'the very genius of war'. Others praised him as 'America's Hannibal.'

It was not all plain sailing. After the capture of Fort Ticonderoga,

Above: Benedict Arnold was hailed as 'America's Hannibal' after the battle of Saratoga. After he changed sides and fought for the British, he was denounced as one of the most infamous traitors in American history.

Arnold led an ill-fated expedition to attack Quebec in December 1775 in a foolhardy attempt to ally the inhabitants of Canada behind the colonial cause. The assault, launched in the teeth of a howling blizzard, was a total failure. Arnold himself was badly wounded in the leg during the course of the early stages of the battle and had to be carried from the field.

By the latter part of 1776, however, Arnold had recovered sufficiently to take up his command again. Having predicted correctly that the British, commanded by General Guy Carleton, were planning to sail down Lake Champlain to invade upper New York, he hastily organized the construction of an American flotilla on the lake. It took the British completely by surprise when, on 11 October, it struck at their invasion fleet near Valcour Bay.

Although the Americans were beaten off, the delay the attack caused proved disastrous for the British. When they finally reached their destination, the campaigning season was nearing its end and winter was setting in fast.

They had no choice but to turn back and retrace their steps to Canada. Arnold's timely action had saved the colonial cause from potential disaster.

Yet Arnold was not an easy man to deal with. He took offence easily and held many of his military colleagues, Congress and the rest of the political establishment in contempt. 'How can Congress allow this army to starve in a land of plenty?' he questioned on one occasion after the legislature had stinted on the money it was prepared to allot for the purchase of military supplies. Congress retaliated by promoting five junior officers over his head.

Arnold immediately protested to Washington about the scurvy way he felt he had been treated. 'Having made every sacrifice of fortune and blood and become a crippled in the service of my country,' he expostulated, 'I little expected to meet the ungrateful returns I have received from my countrymen!' His outburst was almost certainly occasioned by the way he felt he had been treated by General Horatio Gates during the build-up to the battle of Saratoga in autumn 1777.

The two men quarrelled about the best tactics to employ to check the advance of General John Burgoyne's 8,000-strong British army. Arnold was in favour of an all-out assault. The more cautious Gates – his men had nicknamed him 'Granny' because of his tentative leadership in the field – wanted to remain on the defensive. He refused to send Arnold the reinforcements he demanded. Then, when Arnold once again exceeded his authority at Freeman's Farm, Gates relieved him of his command, citing insubordination as the reason for the removal.

Arnold was incandescent with rage. Ignoring Gates' orders – by now the two men were not on speaking terms – he charged into action when the main battle was joined, despite the fact he held no official command. Inspired by his example, the Americans rallied, launching two fierce assaults on the British positions. The latter began to crumble under the pressure.

It was at this moment, with victory in the offing, that Arnold's horse was shot from under him. It fell onto the same leg that had been injured earlier during the assault on Quebec. As a result, Arnold found himself crippled for life. While recovering slowly from the wound, he was even more infuriated when he learned that Gates was claiming all the credit for the decisive American victory and Burgoyne's subsequent surrender.

It was clear that his wound made Arnold unfit for active service, so Washington had him appointed military governor of Philadelphia. Soon rumours started to circulate through the city that he was abusing his position for personal gain. His marriage to the much younger Philadelphia socialite Peggy Shippen was certainly expensive. The two lived lavishly and accumulated substantial debts. These – and his continuing resentment at not having been promoted faster – were probably the catalysts in his decision to turn traitor.

Some believe that Arnold employed Joseph Stansbury, a Loyalist in the pay of the British, to establish communications with Major John Andre, who was General Sir Henry Clinton's aide and head of intelligence. Others say it was Peggy herself who managed to put the two men in touch. The two men first made contact on 10 May 1779. For the next 16 months, Arnold supplied Andre with military secrets in return for the promise of a substantial sum of money and an eventual commission in the British Army after the war.

Among the secrets Arnold divulged was Washington's plan for the Yorktown campaign, and intelligence concerning the strengths and weaknesses of the Continental Army. On 15 July 1780, he offered to engineer the surrender of West Point for what was then the enormous sum of £80,000. Clinton himself confirmed to Andre that he was prepared to authorize the payment once the surrender had taken place. Arnold took over command of the fort on 3 August. The two men conducted their treasonous business in writing, with undercover messengers smuggling letters and documents back and forth

TREACHEROUS BEAUTY

ARNOLD WAS NOT alone in plotting treason. Margaret 'Peggy' Shippen, a vivacious Philadelphian socialite from a Loyalist family who became the widowed Arnold's second wife – he was 38 and she aged only 19 – was probably as guilty. Indeed, the likelihood is that she encouraged him in his treachery.

During the year the British had occupied Philadelphia, Peggy had become close friends with John Andre, a handsome British officer with an eye for the ladies. When she discovered how discontented her husband was with his lot, she covertly managed to contact Andre and put the two men in touch. Andre promised Arnold substantial sums of money in return for military information. The most important items that were handed over were the plans of the key fortress Arnold had been put in command of at West Point.

The plot went awry. Andre was captured and Arnold fled, leaving Peggy and her young baby behind. She feigned hallucinations to get herself off the hook, managing to convince George Washington himself that she had no knowledge of her husband's treachery. Eventually, she made it to New York where she and Arnold were reunited. The two finally took ship for England as the war neared its end. They were never to see America again.

Above: General John Burgoyne surrenders to the Americans after his defeat at the battle of Saratoga. Arnold, who was crippled for life in the battle, played a major part in winning the victory.

between them. As a security precaution, Arnold devised a cipher to ensure the letters' contents remained secret. The key to decoding the messages was to be found in two common reference books of the time – *Blackstone's Commentaries on the Laws of England* and *Nathan Bailey's Dictionary*.

It worked like this. When Arnold composed a letter, he first located the words he wanted in either one of the two books. He then wrote down the page number, the line number, and the number of the word, counting from the left. The three numbers taken together therefore represented the word. As an extra precaution, he and Andre both left certain words unencoded. These words were cleverly chosen to support the pretence that the letters were the work of two merchants, writing to each other about commercial transactions.

On 22 September, Arnold and Andre finally met to iron out the details of the West Point surrender. The American traitor handed over copies of the plans of the fort's defences and told Andre that he had already posted away some of the troops making up its garrison. Then the plot went awry. The following day, while making his way between the British and American lines disguised in civilian clothes, Andre was captured by an American militia patrol. He was still carrying the documents Arnold had given him. Under interrogation, Andre admitted that he had been involved in espionage, his accomplice being an undisclosed American traitor.

It was first decided to send Andre to Arnold, of all people, for further questioning. He and his escort had actually set out for Philadelphia when the order was countermanded. Nevertheless, Arnold got the news of the arrest before Washington. He panicked and fled north down the Hudson River, reached the British sloop *Vulture* and made his way to New York and safety. Andre was not as fortunate. He was tried by court-martial and condemned to death. He was hanged on 2 October.

Arnold soon began fighting for the British. In December 1780, he led a force into Virginia, capturing Richmond and sacking much of the city. He remained in command until May 1781, when Lord Cornwallis took over. His last American action was to attack and take the port of New London, just a few miles from his Connecticut birthplace.

When news of the surrender at Yorktown reached New York, Arnold and his family sailed for London. At first, he was well received, but soon found there was no place for him in the British military establishment. Nor would ministers pay him the money he claimed he was due. The most he got out of them was a lump sum of £6,315 and a pension of £360 a year.

Arnold turned to trade with the West Indies to restore his fortunes – first from Canada and then from the island of Guadeloupe. In Guadeloupe, however, he fell foul of the French, who arrested him on suspicion of spying for the British. He bribed his way out of prison and managed to make his escape. Back in London, his finances went from bad to worse and his health started to decline.

Arnold died on 14 June 1801 at the age of 60. His wife summed up his last years as follows. 'For his own sake, the change is a most happy one', she wrote, 'as the disappointment of all his expectations, with the numerous vexations and mortifications he has endured, had so broken his spirits and destroyed his nerves, that he has been for a long time past incapable of the smallest enjoyment.' It was a sad, but fitting epitaph.

William Wickham

The well-born Yorkshireman spied on the French from his Swiss lair. His activities may have inspired Baroness Orczy to create her legendary hero Sir Percy Blakeney, the 'Scarlet Pimpernel'

LIKE MANY OTHER great spymasters, William Wickham entered the murky world of espionage more by accident than deliberate design. Born into a well-to-do Yorkshire family, he was educated at Harrow and Christ Church, Oxford. It was there that he became close friends with William Wyndham Grenville, a fellow undergraduate who was later to become Lord Grenville. It was Grenville who was to shape the future course of the young Wickham's career.

In 1793, after Louis XVI and Marie Antoinette perished on the guillotine, Britain broke off diplomatic relations with Revolutionary France. Grenville, by this time Foreign Secretary in William Pitt the Younger's government, needed someone he could trust implicitly to get in touch with all the exiled anti-revolutionary factions scattered throughout Europe and at the same time promote monarchist uprisings against the Revolutionary regime in France itself. His old university friend seemed just the man for the job.

FACT FILE

BORN: 11 November 1761, Cottingley, Yorkshire

DIED: 22 October 1840, Brighton, Sussex

MISSION: Between 1794 and 1801, spied on the French, plotting with the Royalists and others to overthrow the French Revolutionary government and to restore the Bourbon monarchy

INTELLIGENCE TECHNIQUES: Codes, ciphers and bribery

FATE: Retired from active life in 1807 after serving as an MP and Chief Secretary for Ireland

LEGACY: Succeeded in keeping Royalist resistance alive for a time, though the uprising he helped to plan in the Vendée department in west central France was a disastrous failure

After Oxford, Wickham had continued his education in Switzerland, moving to Geneva to study civil law at the university there. He had married Eleonore Madeline Bertrand, the daughter of a professor, and became friends with a number of prominent Frenchmen, Swiss and Germans. In Grenville's opinion, no man was better placed to become the eyes and ears of the British government in the Swiss cantons. He also had distinguished himself as Superintendent of Aliens at the Home Office, where he had set a spy to work observing the activities of the radical London Correspondence Society and looking for evidence of sedition.

Britain was not yet officially at war with France, so the government could not afford to be seen to be openly backing the anti-revolutionary cause. Grenville told Wickham that his actual mission must be kept a closely guarded secret, though he would be provided with unlimited funds. Wickham recollected in 1831: 'The nature and object of this mission was considered so secret and confidential that I never appeared at the Foreign

Above: Hastily armed with any weapons they could muster, loyal French republicans take Louis XVI and Marie Antoinette prisoner at Varennes, as depicted in a contemporary British caricature.

Office at all.' As cover, he was appointed aide to the British Ambassador in Berne, Switzerland, and later himself took over as Ambassador.

Over the next seven years – first from Switzerland and then from Swabia, on the German-Swiss border – Wickham helped thousands of fleeing French aristocrats to escape the guillotine. His spies infiltrated the Directory (the French government of the time), several military councils and many political clubs, so that, when secret instructions and orders were despatched to French diplomats, generals and admirals, it was almost certain that they would be scanned by Wickham's ubiquitous eyes.

Perhaps the most ambitious of Wickham's intrigues were his efforts to persuade – or, more likely, bribe – the French general Jean-Charles Pichegru, the commander of the Army of the North and then of the Army of the Rhine and Moselle, to change sides and, together with his troops, join the Prince de Condé, Louis XVI's cousin who had raised a Royalist army and was fighting together with the Austrians on the Rhine. Wickham had already agreed to finance Condé and was behind the raising of a regiment of Swiss volunteers to support the Prince in his campaign.

It became known to Wickham that Pichegru had become disenchanted with the extreme violence displayed by the Jacobins and had indicated that he was prepared to consider abandoning the revolutionary cause. Louis Fouche-Borel, a Swiss barber, was the chosen go-between. He had been recruited by Comte de Montgaillard, one of Condé's most trusted agents. Wickham gave Fouche-Borel £8,000 to pass onto Pichegru, ostensibly to purchase food and other supplies for his soldiers.

Once the French general had got his hand on Wickham's gold, however, he began to vacillate and temporize. It was not yet time, he asserted, for him to make any such move. Wickham had to abandon the plot. In the meantime, the Directory had already started to doubt Pichegru's loyalty. Because of his popularity with his troops, it was impossible to arrest him. In early 1796, he was allowed to retire honourably from his command. Later he entered politics, was caught plotting against Napoleon and, in 1804, was thrown into jail. He died in mysterious circumstances, found strangled in his prison cell.

The Directory had got wind of Wickham's activities as well. At least one unsuccessful attempt was made to kidnap him; in 1797, the Swiss were forced to press for his recall. The last straw as far as the French were

Below: Wickham's network of highly-placed agents in France rescued thousands of French aristocrats from a grisly end by guillotine. Louis XIV, whose moment of death is pictured here, was not so lucky.

concerned, was his discovery of their plan to invade Ireland. Wickham's timely warning enabled the government to suppress an Irish revolt before the French could arrive on the scene.

Back in London, Wickham returned to the Home Office, though he returned to Europe once more in 1799. In 1801, Pitt's ministry fell. Lord Hawkesbury, the new Foreign Secretary, told him that he planned to make him Ambassador either in Vienna or Berlin, but both the Austrians and Prussians refused to agree to the appointment. Perhaps Wickham's reputation as a master-spy had preceded him and both powers feared that he might take up espionage again.

Wickham was not that disappointed. His previous missions, he wrote, had been 'complicated, difficult and laborious beyond belief.' Instead, he went to Ireland as Chief Secretary. He stayed until December 1803, when, troubled by ill-health and disturbed by the government's handling of another Irish rebellion, he resigned. He was never to hold office again.

Wickham had already done more than his duty, as Grenville, for one, had been quick to recognize. In December 1794, he wrote: 'A few words to express to you how completely all the king's servants have been satisfied with the manner in which you have treated the very delicate transaction with which you were entrusted.' It was an elegant tribute to the work of one of Britain's first great master spies.

The 'Great Game'

Upholding the British raj was not without its risks. Political agent Sir Alexander Burnes was killed by an Afghan mob while playing the 'Great Game' to checkmate a threatened Russian advance on India

IT WAS, WROTE a contemporary commentator, 'a war begun for no wise purpose, carried on with a strange mixture of rashness and timidity, brought to a close after suffering and disaster, without much glory attached.' When the Kabul garrison was forced to retire ignominiously back towards India in 1842, more than 16,000 of the soldiers and camp followers who had set out so confidently through the 50-mile-long Bolan Pass two years before were slaughtered.

Among the first to die was Sir Alexander Burnes, hacked to death by an angry mob in the street immediately outside his residence in Kabul. Ironically Burnes was about to take over from Sir William McNaghten as Britain's envoy to the Amir of Afghanistan's court when he met his tragic end.

Even more ironically, he had been in love with the city and its people ever since he had first visited Kabul in 1832. Burnes likened Kabul to an earthly paradise. Its gardens, with their abundance of fruit trees

FACT FILE

BORN: 16 May 1805, Montrose, Scotland

DIED: 2 November 1841, Kabul, Afghanistan

MISSIONS: Surveyed the River Indus and reached Lahore (1831); expedition to Kabul and Bokhara, (1832); expedition to Kabul (1836); returned to Afghanistan as deputy envoy to Sir William McNaghten, 1839

INTELLIGENCE TECHNIQUES: Bribery, mastery of languages, use of disguise

FATE: Killed in 1841 as he tried to escape the angry Afghan mob who attacked his house in Kabul

LEGACY: Coined phrase the 'Great Game', to describe the rivalry between Britain and Russia in Central Asia and along the northwest frontier of India

Left: Alexander Burnes, seen in the native dress he loved to adopt during his exotic travels, soon proved himself an adept player of the 'Great Game', when he was transferred to the elite Indian political department.

and songbirds, reminded him, he said, of England and home. 'There were peaches, plums, apricots, pears, apples, quinces, cherries, walnuts, mulberries, pomegranates and vines', he wrote, ' all growing in one garden. There were also nightingales, blackbirds, thrushes and doves ... and chattering magpies on almost every tree.' Burnes was so taken with the nightingales' song that an Afghan friend arranged to have one delivered to him once he had returned to India. Christened 'the nightingale of a thousand tales', it sang so loudly all night long that it had to be taken out of earshot in order for Burnes to get some sleep.

Burnes had first arrived in India in 1821 at the age of 16 to join the East India Company as a military cadet. Though slightly built and relatively undistinguished-looking, his quick wits, resourcefulness and daring soon caught the eyes of his superiors. So did his natural linguistic skills – he quickly mastered Persian, Arabic and Hindustani as well as some of the lesser-known Indian tongues.

In 1831, promoted from the 1st Bombay Light Infantry to the elite Political Department, Burnes successfully surveyed 700 miles of the River Indus, getting as far as Lahore, the capital of the Punjab. Still aged only 26, the young Burnes was obviously destined to reach the top. Indeed, no less a personage than Lord William Bentinck, the Governor-General of Bengal, commended him for the 'zeal, diligence and intelligence' with which he had carried out such a delicate task.

What really made Burnes' reputation was his second intelligence-gathering mission the following year. He went disguised as a native. Having discarded 'the useless paraphernalia of civilization', he wrote, 'we threw away all our European clothes and adopted, without reserve, the costume of the Asiatic ... groaning under ponderous turbans'. Burnes' initial destination was Afghanistan, where he struck up a friendship with Dost Mohammed, the kingdom's ruler. From there, he continued through the passes of the Hindu Kush and crossed the Rover Oxus into Central Asia to reach the fabled Khanate of Bokhara. He then pressed on across the Turcoman Desert and to the shores of the Caspian Sea, finally returning to Bombay via Persia.

The intelligence Burnes gleaned was considered important enough for him to be sent back to London to report in person. Christened 'Bokhara' Burnes by the press, he was lionized by high society and granted audiences with the Prime Minister and King William IV. He was even introduced to

Princess Victoria, the 14-year-old heir apparent to the throne. She thought his tales 'very interesting'. Burnes cemented his reputation with his *Travels into Bokhara*, which was an instant bestseller.

Burnes had written most of his book during the voyage home to England. He had also penned four secret reports – one military, one political and two on the commercial prospects and topography of the Central Asian region. Of the four, the military report was the most immediately significant.

Above: Dost Mohammed, pictured with his son, had been schooled in deceit and treachery; these skills helped to propel him onto the Afghan throne in 1826 after Shah Shujah had been ousted.

Above: Dost Mohammed's early friendship with Burnes was impaired as a result of the Afghan ruler's intrigues with the Russians.

In it, Burnes argued that it would be just as dangerous to allow Kabul to fall into hostile hands as it would Herat, the guardian of one of the traditional gateways into India. Indeed, he calculated that it would take a well-equipped Russian army just a month to get from Balkh to Kabul. Even the courageous Afghans could not hope to defend their capital for long if confronted by a determined Russian force.

Dost Mohammed knew this, too. While welcoming Burnes effusively on his return to Kabul – Lord Auckland, the newly-appointed Governor-General of India, had ordered Burnes back there in November 1836 – the Afghan ruler secretly put out feelers to the Russians. Tsar Nicholas I's response was instant. Captain Yan Vitkevich was dispatched to open talks with the Afghan ruler.

The Russian was around the same age as Burnes and possessed many of the same personal qualities. A member of an aristocratic Lithuanian family, he had fallen foul of the Russian authorities when, as a 17-year-old student in Warsaw, he got involved with the Polish nationalist movement. He was forcibly exiled to Siberia as a Russian Army conscript. To occupy himself during the long months of boredom, he set about mastering Central Asia's languages. Soon, his linguistic skills and other talents attracted the attention of his seniors. He was promoted lieutenant and tasked with gathering intelligence among the Muslim tribes of the frontier hinterlands. He was so successful in this that General Perovsky, the Russian commander-in-chief at Orenburg, seconded him to his personal staff, saying that no other officer knew more about the region than his new aide.

Others thought the same. Vitkevich was summoned to St Petersburg, where he was personally briefed on his Afghan mission by Count Nesselrode, the Russian Foreign Minister. He then made for Tehran to confer with

Count Simonich, the Russian Ambassador to the newly-crowned Shah of Persia. On Christmas Eve 1837, he rode into Kabul. Burnes, who knew of his impending arrival, promptly invited him to Christmas dinner the next day.

The following weeks were crucial as Burnes and Vitkevich fought for Dost Mohammed's ear. At first, the Russian was the underdog, but then Auckland intervened to cut the ground from under Burnes' feet. He sent an ultimatum to Kabul. Against Burnes' advice, Auckland warned Dost Mohammed that, should he conclude an alliance of any kind with the Russians, the British would intervene and remove him forcibly from the throne. Furthermore, Auckland insisted that Dost Mohammed renounce his claims to Peshawar, which the Afghan ruler had been trying to persuade the British to let him annex for some time.

Through no direct fault of his own, Burnes had lost the battle of wits. On 27 April 1838, he left Kabul for India. Vitkevich was not far behind him. London now put direct pressure on St Petersburg to force his recall. They demanded Simonvich's removal from Teheran into the bargain.

What happened next is still something of a mystery. In St Petersburg, Vitkevich reported to the Foreign Ministry, apparently expecting to be congratulated on his achievements. Instead, it appears that Nesselrode cold-shouldered him. Back in his hotel room, Vitkevich blew his brains out – but not before setting fire to his papers, including all the intelligence he had taken such pains to collect. Count Simonich was officially disgraced. The 'Great Game' had claimed two victims.

Meanwhile in Calcutta, Auckland was deciding on whether to intervene militarily. Sir William McNaghten, the Secretary to the Political Department, argued forcibly that the British should back the deposed Shah Shujah, who had been living in India in exile for the last 30 years. Auckland eventually agreed. Having secured London's backing, he ordered the soldiers of the Army of the Indus to prepare for action. McNaghten was to go with them as emissary to Shah Shujah's court. Burnes was his deputy.

In December 1838, the great advance began. Slowly but surely, the Army of the Indus pushed forward, though its progress was less speedy than had been expected. It was harassed by Afghan tribesmen and frequently ran short of food. Nevertheless, on 25 April, Kandahar, Afghanistan's southern capital, fell without a shot being fired. After the great fortress of Ghahzi was stormed, Dost Mohammed fled north to Bokhara.

Kabul was occupied on 6 August and Shah Shujah reinstalled upon the Afghan throne. The expedition seemed to be a total success, but General Sir John Keane, the commander-in-chief of the Army of the Indus, had forebodings of future disaster. 'I cannot but congratulate you on quitting this country', he remarked to one of his officers who was about to return to India, 'for, mark my words, it will not be long before there is here some signal catastrophe'. Keane, too, was on the point of leaving Afghanistan. He was replaced by General William Elphinstone – an indecisive, tired old man who was crippled by gout.

McNaghten, who was counting the moments until he could return to India to become Governor-General of Bombay and Burnes, who was set to take over from him, were more sanguine. They were blind to the growing animosity that was inexorably building up towards the British occupiers. Though Dost Mohammed himself surrendered in December 1840 and was packed off to exile in India, the danger continued to mount. Major Henry Rawlinson, the Political Agent at Kandahar, was one of the first to sound the alarm. 'The feeling against us is daily on the increase', he warned in August 1841, 'and I apprehend a succession of disturbances'. Major Eldred Pottinger, operating among the tribes to the north of Kabul, concurred. Their chieftains, he warned, were readying themselves for an uprising. McNaghten dismissed both men as alarmists – 'croakers' in the idiom of the day.

It took just one spark to kindle the blaze. On 1 November, Burnes was warned by Mohan Lal, his Kashmiri assistant, that an attempt was going to be made to kill him that night. Burnes was possibly the most unpopular of all the British occupiers. Many Afghans believed that he had masterminded the invasion of their homeland after spying out their land under the pretext of friendship. His numerous love affairs with Afghan women had only served to deepen this hostility.

Even more to the point, Burnes had chosen to reside in a large, somewhat secluded house in the centre of the city, rather than move out to live with the garrison in the cantonments to the north. This left him isolated and vulnerable. Nevertheless, he turned down Lal's advice to take refuge in the cantonments, asking simply for his Sepoy guard to be reinforced that night.

As dusk fell, the mob began to gather. The ringleaders were all Afghans Burnes had personally offended. As the numbers swelled – many drawn by the rumour that the house next door housed the garrison treasury – the situation

grew worse. Telling the Sepoys to hold their fire, Burnes harangued the mob from a balcony to gain time for troops from the garrison to rescue him and his companions, who included his brother Charles, visiting Kabul on leave from his regiment in India, and Major William Broadfoot, his political assistant.

Broadfoot was the first to die, shot by a single sniper in the crowd. Other Afghans set fire to the house, which was soon ablaze. Burnes, realizing that no help was coming, finally ordered the Sepoys to open fire, while he and his brother tried to make a getaway. The loyal Mohan Lal, watching from a nearby rooftop, saw Burnes' brother die. He 'came out into the garden', Lal recorded, 'and killed about six persons before he was cut to pieces'. No one, however, saw Burnes killed. According to one account, he was betrayed to the mob by a traitor in his own household while trying to make his escape in disguise. He, too, was hacked to pieces.

McNaghten and Elphinstone had dithered about sending help until it was far too late. They, too, were to perish. McNaghten was killed by the Afghan chieftains with whom he was attempting to negotiate a safe conduct out of the city for the garrison. Elphinstone died in Afghan captivity. His troops and their camp-followers were massacred as, two months later they finally tried to fall back to Jalalabad, 90 miles away. Only one Briton and a handful of others escaped the catastrophe.

Below: Dr. William Brydon, sole survivor of the massacre at Futtehabad, struggles across the plain to Jalalabad and safety. It was he who broke the news of the disaster that had overtaken the Army of the Indus to a horrified nation.

Belle Boyd

The 'Siren of the Shenandoah', a Confederate spy who was said to be 'the fastest girl in Virginia, or anywhere else for that matter'

MUSKET BALLS PIERCED her clothing and an artillery shell exploded just 20 yards away as the 18-year-old Southern girl dashed towards Stonewall Jackson's Confederate troops on 23 May 1862. Her crinoline swayed as she ran, her long, dark-blue dress and fancy white apron might have been ripped, but she was determined to get her message through. The way ahead was almost clear, and if the men charged now the battle would be won. It was Belle Boyd's most famous exploit, and it made her name – for good or for bad – throughout the length of war-torn America.

This was not the first time that Belle Boyd had been in the news, however. She was born Isabelle Marie Boyd on 9 May 1844, in Martinsburg, Virginia (later West Virginia), to a family wealthy enough to sent her to Mount Washington Female College in Baltimore, an academy for ladies 'of gentle birth.' After graduating in 1860, perhaps less of a tomboy than she is reported to have been before, she became a debutante in Washington.

FACT FILE

BORN: 15 May 1844, Bunker Hill, Virginia (now West Virginia)

DIED: 11 June 1900, Kilbourn (now Wisconsin Dells), Wisconsin

MISSION: Self-imposed: to help the Confederates in any possible way, but primarily by passing messages between their generals, helping to supply provisions and arms and relaying any useful information about troop dispositions

INTELLIGENCE TECHNIQUES: Coquettishness, vamping, brazenness and complete openness about what she was doing

FATE: Arrested three times, imprisoned twice, ended her career recounting her exploits on the stage

LEGACY: A heroine of the South

Above: General Thomas 'Stonewall' Jackson, one of the Confederacy's most able commanders, who Belle Boyd supplied with the intelligence he needed to capture Front Royal as his army advanced through Virginia.

Previous page: An apparent example of demure Southern womanhood, Belle Boyd would prove to be one of boldest and most resourceful Confederate spies.

The outbreak of the Civil War put a stop to Belle's fun-loving life. She returned to Martinsburg, which was captured by Union forces in July 1861. The victorious troops became drunk and started to ransack the town, and they particularly targeted the South-loving Boyd household, which had Confederate flags on display. Furious, they tried to fly a Union flag over its door, only for Belle's mother to tell them, 'Men, every member of my household will die before that flag shall be raised over us.' Curses and threats followed, until Belle Boyd, who was just 17 at the time, stepped forward and shot Frederick Martin, of the Seventh Pennsylvania Volunteers, dead.

Extraordinarily, Belle got away with it. She was arrested, but a Federal investigation into the shooting found that she 'had done exactly right.' But how, in the midst of war, did they come to this conclusion? The clue lies in Belle herself. Though not strictly speaking beautiful – one journalist said, 'It would be ungallant to report ... that her longish nose and protruding teeth made her a bit horse-faced' – she had a superb figure and was always immaculately dressed. And, rather like Scarlet O'Hara in *Gone With the Wind*, she combined charm, vivacity and coquettishness to devastating effect and had a way of making men want to protect her. In short, she charmed her way out of the situation – it was a lesson that she was to put to good use over the coming years.

Encouraged by her let-off, but still staunchly behind the Confederate cause, Belle started to use her charms to further effect. The Union troops were watching her, of course, but she is said to have managed to wrap one of their officers, a Captain Daniel Keily, round her little finger and extract secrets from him. Her notes were hidden in a watch case and carried through the Union lines to be delivered to the Confederates by her slave, Eliza Creswell.

As the war progressed, Belle became increasingly bold. She started to carry messages between Confederate generals, riding immaculately on a tall horse over rough ground. She also collected weapons – sometimes stealing them from Union camps – and set up arms dumps that the Confederates

THE SPY ON THE STAGE

EXILED IN LONDON, Belle's funds were dwindling and she was falling on hard times. To make matters worse, Sam Hardinge died not long after their marriage. *Belle Boyd in Camp and Prison*, a stirring account of her adventures had been published in May 1865, just before his death, which relieved her situation, but the relief was only temporary – and now she had a daughter, Grace. There was nothing for it, she thought, but to go on the stage.

Belle, now 22, made her debut at The Theatre Royal, Manchester in 1866, in a dramatic role. But she saw that her future lay back in America, and by the end of the year she had returned there and opened at Ben de Bar's Theatre in St Louis, before moving to The 14th Street Theatre in New York – but only for one night. It was time for Belle to reinvent herself, and she is next heard of acting in Cincinnati under the name 'Nina Benjamin'. Again, the critics were unimpressed, and she retired from the dramatic stage in 1869. (Ironically, five years later *Belle Lamar*, a play by the noted Irish dramatist – or, rather melodramatist – Dion Boucicault, opened in New York; it was all about Belle's own exploits and would have been ideal for her.)

A John Swainston Hammond, a British officer in the Crimean War who had also fought for the Confederacy but was now a merchant, had been in the audience for one of Belle's last appearances; he was smitten by her and the two soon married. The Hammonds, together with Grace, two new daughters, Byrd and Marie Isabelle and a son, John, lived happily enough it seemed, until 1884, when Belle was granted a divorce. It was time for a new husband, and a return to the stage.

In 1885, Belle, now 41, married a 24-year-old actor called Nathaniel Rue High who played juvenile leads. With four children to support and in a precarious occupation, the couple decided to try a new tack. Unlike any other spy, and according to the policy of complete openness that she had espoused through her spying career, Belle and High took to the road with a 'Story of battlefields and the sea; dangerous rides and missions; the outwitting of Federal officers; captures, sentences, imprisonments, reprieves'. By another account, Belle went on stage '... in an attractive uniform of Confederate grey, wearing a broad, low-crowned hat with a large, flowing black plume ... before a stage background of battle and strife', before starting an emotional dramatic recital.

The show was a great success and played all over America – so much so that Belle had to carry documents proving that she was the real Belle Boyd, because there were so many impersonators. It all ended in Wisconsin on 11 June 1900, when she died from a heart attack at only 56. The feisty Siren of the Shenandoah had thrilled America for the last time.

could draw on. But what was perhaps her finest hour came when she was staying near her parents' new house, in Front Royal, Warren County, Virginia, on May 23, 1862 – 'near' because Union troops had requisitioned it. Belle remembered that there was a knothole in an outside wall and bent her ear to it to listen to Union officers making their defence plans in the face of the advance of General Stonewall Jackson's Army of the Valleys.

Armed with this vital information, and knowing that Front Royal was now lightly defended, she ran to the Confederates, waving her white bonnet as she ran as the signal to advance, to meet Major Harry Kyd Douglas, one of Jackson's staff officers.

'Oh Harry, Give me time to catch my breath. I knew it must be Stonewall when I heard the first gun. Go back quick and tell him that the Yankee force is very small – one regiment of Maryland infantry, several pieces of artillery and several companies of cavalry . . . . Tell him to charge right down and he will catch them all. I must hurry back [she blew Douglas a kiss] . . . . Goodbye. My love to the boys.'

By now, Belle enjoyed the Confederates' complete trust. The 1st Maryland Infantry, CSA and Major Roberdeau Wheat's Louisiana 'Tigers' battalion charged forward and took Front Royal.

The Union newspapers were not impressed. Belle Boyd was made out to be a wretched scarlet woman, no better than an ' accomplished prostitute', and called her, variously:

'The Amazon of Secession' ... ' The Siren of the Shenandoah' ... ' La Belle Rebelle' ... ' The Rebel Joan of Arc' and ' The fastest girl in Virginia, or anywhere else for that matter.'

Undaunted, Belle continued her work. She carried messages and even spent time in Union camps, wheedling information out of the officers she charmed. She became more and more open about what she was doing: one report has her in a Union camp wearing a grey frock coat made of wool, a butternut kepi, a velvet headband carrying the seven stars of the Confederacy, and a pair of shoulder straps giving her rank as ' Lieutenant Colonel, Fifth Virginia Regiment, Confederate Army.' It seems extraordinary that she was allowed to get away with it.

But it was all too good to be true. Inevitably, there was talk in the corridors of Washington, where people were immune to Belle's charms. Allan Pinkerton, who went on to found the eponymous national detective agency, opened a dossier on her and reported his suspicions to the Union's Secretary of War,

Opposite: Allan Pinkerton, President Lincoln and Union General John A. McClernand confer after the bloody battle of Antietam in 1862. Pinkerton suspected Belle Boyd of spying, right from the start.

Edward Stanton. It was only a few months after Front Royal that a Union spy posing as a Confederate officer took a letter that she had intended for Stonewall Jackson and arrested her. "All's fair in love and war', she said. Belle was sent to prison, where she was encouraged to repeat the Union's Oath of Allegiance – doing so would have ensured her freedom.

Her response was swift and to the point, 'Tell Mr Stanton from me, I hope that when I commence the oath of allegiance to the United States Government my tongue may cleave to the roof of my mouth and that if I shall ever sign one line that will show to the world that I owe the United States Government the slightest allegiance, I hope my arm may fall paralyzed by my side.'

But prison was to prove a temporary setback. Soon enough, Belle had charmed her way out, though banished to the South. This did not deter her: essentially, she carried on as before. She used her Southern charms to persuade all manner of Union generals and officials to sign passes that would allow her to move freely from place to place to help the Confederate cause.

Eventually, Stanton had had enough. In July 1863 he ordered Colonel Kellog, the Provost Marshall, to arrest her and she was sent back to the Old Capitol Prison in Washington. Her situation there seems to have been rather mysterious and certainly unconventional. She was paroled to walk in a nearby square, for example, and managed to communicate with other prisoners by pushing notes through holes dug in the thin walls, and with the outside world through notes crammed into a small rubber ball that was thrown in and out of her cell window. And, yet again, she was released – this time on condition that she did not cross into the Union lines for the rest of the war. (It was rumoured that Stanton had wanted her to be shot, but that President Lincoln had intervened to grant her clemency.)

For a while, Belle travelled around the Southern states in a desultory way, though she was feted wherever she went. But then she hit on another way of assisting the cause: to carry despatches from President Jefferson Davis (of the Confederacy) to the Southern community in London, which provided it with invaluable supplies, money and informal diplomatic services. She set sail on the Confederate blockade runner *Greyhound* from Wilmington, North Carolina, in April 1864. The Yankees knew perfectly well what was going on, however, and on Belle's 20th birthday the *Greyhound* was intercepted and forced to surrender. Belle, who had sailed under a false name, was soon unmasked and her despatches confiscated.

A Lieutenant Sam Hardinge was put in charge of the prize, and Belle quickly deployed her charms. Within weeks, he had proposed, only to be given a non-committal answer. It seems that Belle then duped him into allowing the *Greyhound's* master, Captain Henry, to escape. Yet she was released again, this time banished to Canada, and warned that she would be shot if she set foot in America again – Hardinge was dismissed and sent to prison for a time.

From Canada, Belle took a boat to England – even if she no longer had the despatches she could still remember what they contained. She made her way to London, where Confederate supporters made much of her. A few months later, Sam Hardinge had joined her and they were married in St James's Church in Piccadilly, on 25 August 1864 in front of a congregation packed with Confederates and sensation seekers. Soon, however, Belle was to be a rebel without a cause, as the American Civil War ended in the Confederates' surrender in April 1865. Her spying days were over.

Above: The Old Capitol Prison in Washington was where Belle Boyd was detained after her arrest on 29 July 1862. Despite her refusal to recant her Confederate views, she was freed within months.

The Dreyfus Case

In October 1894, Captain Alfred Dreyfus, a rising star of France's General Staff, was arrested and accused of spying for Germany. His subsequent condemnation was one of the most infamous miscarriages of justice in French history

ON THE MORNING of 5 January 1895 in the courtyard of the École Militaire in Paris, a dramatic event took place. It was the setting chosen by the French Army's High Command for the ritual degradation of Captain Alfred Dreyfus, the only Jew on the General Staff, who had been convicted of spying for Germany.

The ceremony began at 8:45am, when Dreyfus, escorted by four fellow-artillery officers, was led out into the courtyard, where picked representatives from every branch of the armed forces were drawn up to witness the spectacle. Drums beat slowly as Dreyfus was marched to the centre of the courtyard, where General Paul Darras and the tubby little clerk of the court-martial that had condemned him were waiting. The drums stopped and the clerk read out the judgement. Barras then turned towards Dreyfus and addressed him.

FACT FILE

BORN: 9 October 1859, Mulhouse, Alsace

DIED: 12 July 1935, Paris

MISSION: To prove he was not guilty of spying for Germany, an offence for which he was court-martialled and sentenced to life imprisonment on Devil's Island; it would take 12 years

INTELLIGENCE TECHNIQUES: Forgery

FATE: After his vindication in 1906, Dreyfus was re-admitted to the army and served with distinction in World War I. He retired and died peacefully at the age of 75

LEGACY: The Dreyfus Affair, as it became known, polarized French public opinion. Split between Dreyfusards and anti-Dreyfusards, the country at one time came near to civil war

Le Petit Journal

SUPPLÉMENT ILLUSTRÉ

Le Petit Journal
CHAQUE JOUR 5 CENTIMES
Le Supplément illustré
CHAQUE SEMAINE 5 CENTIMES

Huit pages : CINQ centimes

ABONNEMENTS

	TROIS MOIS	SIX MOIS	UN AN
PARIS	1 fr.	2 fr.	3 fr. 50
DÉPARTEMENTS	1 fr.	2 fr.	4 fr.
ÉTRANGER	1 50	2 50	5 fr.

Cinquième année   DIMANCHE 23 DÉCEMBRE 1894   Numéro 214

Le capitaine Dreyfus devant le conseil de guerre

'Dreyfus', the general pronounced, 'you are unworthy to bear arms. In the name of the President of the Republic, you are hereby degraded.' Dreyfus called out in reply, 'Soldiers, an innocent man is being degraded! Soldiers, an innocent man is being dishonoured! I am innocent, I swear that I am innocent, I remain worthy of serving in the army. Long live France! Long live the army!'

Sergeant-Major Bouxin, one of the tallest men in the French Army, stepped forward. He tore Dreyfus' insignia of rank and his epaulettes off his uniform's tunic. Then he ripped the red stripes from his trousers. Finally, he drew Dreyfus' sword from its scabbard and broke it in two over his knee. Dreyfus shouted again, 'Long live France! I am innocent! I swear it on the heads of my wife and children!' His uniform in tatters, Dreyfus was marched smartly off the parade ground. As the 20,000-strong crowd outside the barred gates and behind the protective railings of the École Militaire caught sight of him, they began to boo, hiss and shout 'coward, Judas, traitor' and 'dirty Jew'.

The degradation was over. Dreyfus was taken promptly to La Santé prison to await transportation to Devil's Island, the malaria-ridden penal colony off the coast of South America which was to be specially re-opened to house him. He was, said *Le Petit Journal*, 'no longer a man, he is a number on a chain gang'. His sentence was imprisonment for life with no prospect of parole.

With Dreyfus' degradation complete, almost everybody was sure the case was at an end. However, Lucie, his wife, was still convinced that he was innocent. So, too, was Mathieu Dreyfus, his elder brother, who told Colonel Sandhert, the head of the Statistical Section, a key intelligence unit at the Ministry of War, that he would devote his 'entire life and family fortune' to getting at the truth.

Outside the family, few shared this belief. One of them was Joseph Gilbert, a doctor from Le Havre, who, at one time, had been the family physician to Félix Faure, now the President of France. Gilbert took advantage of his friendship with Faure to raise the question of Dreyfus' guilt. The exasperated President dismissed his friend's doubts. 'Dreyfus is guilty', he assured him.

'There can be no doubt on that score.' Faure continued: 'To set your mind at rest, I will tell you that he was not condemned on the facts that came

Previous page: Dreyfus stands before his military judges during his first court-martial for supplying military secrets to Germany.

out during the hearing, but upon the production of a document which was not shown to him or to M. Demonge (Dreyfus' lawyer) for reasons of state.'

Gilbert and Mathieu Dreyfus were appalled by the revelation. Deliberately withholding evidence from the accused broke one of the most fundamental rules of justice. There was still more to come. Commandant Georges Picquart, the ailing Sandhert's successor as head of the Statistical Section, now got involved in the case.

Strictly speaking, Picquart was not a Dreyfusard. In fact, he seems to have disliked the man. When he was his instructor at the Ecole Militaire, he had given him low marks and apologized to one of his colleagues on the teaching staff 'for having given him that Jew, Dreyfus'. It was a shocking discovery he made when he took over the Statistical Section that

THE WHISTLE-BLOWER

UNLIKE BRADLEY MANNING and Edward Snowden, his 21st-century counterparts, Commandant Georges Picquart, the French army officer who gathered the fresh evidence that proved Dreyfus not to be guilty, was an establishment man to the core. What changed his mind about Dreyfus' guilt was a chance discovery he made some months after the latter's conviction.

Picquart had just been appointed head of the so-called Statistical Section, a tiny intelligence unit that had compiled the evidence that led to Dreyfus being convicted. Marie Bastian, one of its top agents working as a cleaner in the German Embassy in Paris, had already purloined the discarded memorandum that sealed Dreyfus' fate. Now she secured the scraps of a draft letter-telegram that Colonel Maximilian Schwartzkoppen, the military attaché, had torn to pieces and thrown into his wastepaper basket. When pieced together, the telegram revealed that Commandant Marie-Charles-Ferdinand Walsin Esterhazy, another French officer, was selling secrets to the Germans as well.

Esterhazy was put under surveillance. Picquart ordered his letters to be intercepted and compared the handwriting with the crucial note that had clinched the case against Dreyfus. To his consternation, it was identical. He then examined the contents of the entire Dreyfus file. Much of the other evidence it contained also looked fabricated.

Picquart took his concerns to his superiors. He was told to forget them. When he persisted in his investigation, he was relieved of his command and posted abroad. Still determined to prove Dreyfus innocent, he leaked his new evidence to the president of the Senate and then to Émile Zola, the famous novelist. Picquart was promptly dismissed from the army, denounced as a forger and locked up in solitary confinement for more than a year.

After Dreyfus was finally vindicated in 1906, Picquart rejoined the army, was promoted and, that autumn, became Minister of War. He held the post for three years. In January 1914, he died as a result of a riding accident sustained while commanding the 2nd Army Corps. Many said he was a hero for what he had done. A substantial number of his fellow officers, however, never forgave him for what they saw as his disloyalty to his comrades-in-arms.

convinced him Dreyfus had been falsely accused. Torn-up pieces of a draft letter-telegram – a *petit bleu* as such things were known – recovered by a French undercover agent from a wastepaper basket at the German Embassy revealed the identity of another possible spy. He was Commandant Marie-Charles-Ferdinand Walsin Esterhazy. Comparing Esterhazy's handwriting with the note Dreyfus was supposed to have written, it was clear to Picquart that had all been written by the same man.

Yet when Picquart revealed what he had discovered to his superiors, there was consternation in the army high command. There could be no climb down – too many high reputations would be at stake if it was admitted that, after all, Dreyfus was an innocent man. Instead, what was initiated was a giant cover-up.

Picquart was posted away from Paris – first to eastern France and then to North Africa. His erstwhile subordinates in the Statistical Section, all of whom had been implicated in preparing the false evidence that had convicted Dreyfus, kept silent. One, indeed, went further. On 1 November 1896, Commandant Hubert Henry, the third-in-command of the Statistical Section, set to work fabricating a new document that would once and for all establish Dreyfus's guilt beyond a shadow of a doubt.

Henry had in his possession a letter from Major Alessandro Panizzardi, the Italian military attaché, to his German counterpart – and lover – Schwartzkoppen. The contents of the letter were innocuous enough until Henry, aided by his wife and possibly an expert forger, started doctoring them. The new version read as follows: 'My dear friend. I have read that a Deputy is to ask questions about Dreyfus. If someone in Rome asks for new explanations, I shall say I never had any dealings with the Jew. If someone asks you, say the same, for no one must know what happened with him. Alessandro.'

From the anti-Dreyfusard point of view, Henry had set to work in the nick of time, for now the crucial note Dreyfus was alleged to have written became public property. A photograph of it appeared mysteriously in *Le Matin*. The high command suspected Picquart of having leaked it, though he denied the charge. Its great fear was that someone would recognize the handwriting as Esterhazy's – and that was exactly what happened. Mathieu Dreyfus had enlarged photographs of the note plastered on advertising billboards throughout Paris, along with more pictures showing samples

of his brother's handwriting. Jacques de Castro, a Parisian stockbroker, saw one of the billboards. He immediately recognized the handwriting as being that of Esterhazy, a one-time client of his, and arranged a meeting with the elder Dreyfus to tell him his news.

Dreyfus immediately wrote to Jean-Baptiste Billot, the Minister of War, to denounce Esterhazy as the traitor. But Esterhazy was already proving difficult to handle. Balked of the promotion he considered his due, he threatened to leave the army and 'tell a story that will create a

Above: Convinced that Dreyfus was innocent and a victim of a military conspiracy, Émile Zola, France's greatest novelist, entered the lists as a Dreyfusard in 1898.

scandal throughout the world'. Then, he received an anonymous letter – in fact concocted by Major Ferdinand du Paty de Clam, the man who had arrested Dreyfus, and Henry – warning him of 'what those scoundrels (the Dreyfus family and Picquart) plan to do to ruin you.'

The traitor panicked. He went to Schwartzkoppen and demanded that he help him. Otherwise, the attaché would be expelled from France in disgrace and he, Esterhazy, would take Dreyfus' place on Devil's Island. Schwartzkoppen refused. The increasingly-desperate Esterhazy had more luck with his fellow-officers in the French Army. He was told that he had 'powerful protectors who wanted to save him.' Buoyed up by this support, Esterhazy demanded to be court-martialled himself. If he was acquitted, he and his protectors reasoned, not only would he be vindicated. Dreyfus' guilt would be established once and for all.

The court-martial convened on 10 January 1898. It was a put-up job from start to finish. The seven judges unanimously acquitted Esterhazy of all the charges against him. As soon as their verdict was announced, rapturous cheering broke out in the courtroom. Picquart and Mathieu Dreyfus were jostled and jeered as they tried to leave. As for Esterhazy, he was greeted with cries of 'Long live the army', 'Long live Esterhazy' and 'Long live the martyr of the Jews!' The next day, Picquart was arrested and charged with revealing military secrets to a civilian.

Just when it seemed that the fortunes of the Dreyfusards had reached their nadir, Émile Zola, France's bestselling author, came to their rescue. He penned a vitriolic open letter, titled *J'accuse* (I Accuse), which he addressed to Félix Faure, still President of the Republic, and had also had the letter published in *L'Aurore*, Georges Clemenceau's newspaper. Not only did Zola proclaim Dreyfus' innocence – he named and shamed all the guilty parties who, he alleged, had conspired to put the wronged Dreyfus behind bars. He ended by inviting all those he had denounced to sue him – if they dared.

The government had no choice. It sued both Zola and Alexandre Perrenx, the managing editor of *L'Aurore,* for criminal libel. The libel was the accusation that, in acquitting Esterhazy, the judges had acted 'under orders'. Zola was found guilty and sentenced to a year's imprisonment (Perrenx got four months). When he appealed, the Court of Appeals found for him, but only on a legal technicality.

Above: Zola's open letter to Félix Faure, the President of the Republic, was splashed across the front page of *L'Aurore.* Zola wrote that Faure's 'nights would be haunted by the spectre of an innocent man' – if he did not speak out and name names.

The government tried to sue again. This time, the charge against the writer was defamation and the sentence was the same. By the time it was handed down, however, Zola had left France for Britain. He would remain there in exile for the next 11 months.

Outside France, the conviction was considered a disgrace. 'Zola's true crime has been in daring to rise to defend the truth and civil liberty,' wrote *The Times* of London. To put an end to the protests, Godefroy Cavaignac, the new Minister of War, now made a fatal miscalculation. Totally ignorant of Henry's underhand activities, he quoted from the forged Panizzardi letter that mentioned Dreyfus' name in a speech he made in the Chamber of Deputies. Shortly after that, Captain Louis Cinguet, re-examining the Dreyfus dossier on Cavaignac's orders, detected the letter was a fake.

Cavaignac was an honest man. He had already ordered Esterhazy's discharge from the army for 'habitual misconduct'. Now, he summoned Henry for interrogation. Under his persistent questioning, Henry cracked. Cavaignac ordered his immediate arrest. He was taken to the fortress of Mont-Valerien, where he cut his own throat in his cell.

With Henry's suicide, doubts about Dreyfus' guilt multiplied. Even Henri Brisson, the Prime Minister, joined the ranks of the doubters. He told Lucie Dreyfus to apply for a judicial review of the case. Even though Brisson's government had fallen before the review could take place, there was no stopping it. The Cour de Cassation ordered a new trial.

Dreyfus was brought back to France from Devil's Island in June 1899 to face a second court-martial – this time at Rennes in Brittany. While the Dreyfusards believed that an acquittal was certain, the anti-Dreyfusards had a final card to play. By a majority of five to two, the judges found Dreyfus guilty again, with the caveat that there were 'extenuating circumstances' which lessened the severity of the crime. He was sentenced to ten years' detention.

Pierre Waldeck-Rousseau, France's new premier, was not the only one to be amazed by the verdict. The conviction sparked off widespread protests, especially abroad. The World's Fair, which France was scheduled to hold in 1900, was threatened with a boycott. Queen Victoria herself expressed her sympathy for 'that poor martyr Dreyfus'.

Waldeck-Rousseau could not leave matters as they were. After protracted negotiations, Dreyfus was persuaded not to appeal against the verdict. In return, on 19 September, he was granted a presidential pardon. Waldeck-Rousseau then proceeded to grant an amnesty to everyone else connected with the Dreyfus Case.

Many Dreyfusards, however, were not content to accept the compromise. They demanded nothing less than their hero's total rehabilitation. In 1904, they forced the reopening of the case yet again.

The verdict of the Cour de Cassation was not delivered until 12 July 1906. The Rennes verdict was overturned, and Dreyfus was finally and formally declared to be an innocent man. 'I had never doubted that justice and truth would eventually triumph against deception and crime,' he wrote. 'What sustained me was the unshakeable faith that France would one day proclaim my innocence to the world.'

Opposite: Zola was viciously caricatured as the 'King of Pigs' for his outburst. The anti-Dreyfusards were furious that the writer had attacked the army's High Command.

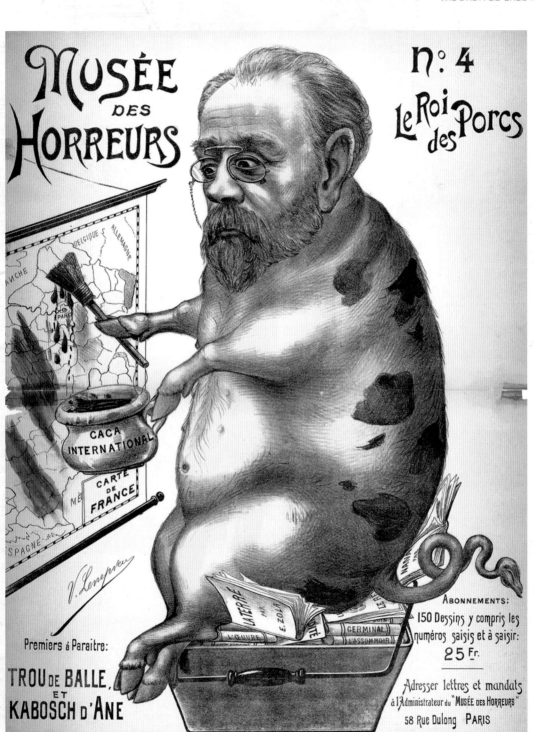

Mata Hari

The Dutch exotic dancer and seductress who, allegedly, played France and Germany against each other during World War I – with fatal results

A FLAMBOYANT FANTASIST and a 'daddy's girl' as a child, who was given a miniature carriage hauled by two goats when she was six, Mata Hari's teenage years and early adulthood were turbulent to say the least. Her once well-off father became bankrupt and left home when she was 13; her Javanese mother, Antje, died when she was 15; aged 17, she was abused at teacher training college; and at 19 she married a 39-year-old diabetic, rheumatic and, probably, syphilitic military man who she met through a newspaper advert.

It was hardly a recipe for a stable, conventional, happy life; that was something that Mata Hari was never to enjoy. Instead, having no money and fewer prospects, she became first, a wife, next an exotic dancer, then a courtesan and finally a spy.

Margaretha Geertruida Zelle, known to her family as 'M'greet', was born in Leeuwarden, The Netherlands, on 7 August 1876, to a well-off hatter and oil investor. Until she was 13, she enjoyed all the benefits of a privileged childhood, with expensive

FACT FILE

BORN: 7 August 1876, Leeuwarden, The Netherlands, as Margaretha Geertruida Zelle

DIED: 15 October 1917, by firing squad at Vincennes, outside Paris, France

MISSION: To extract intelligence from German military and political officials for the benefit of the French, and, allegedly, vice versa for the Germans

INTELLIGENCE TECHNIQUES: Exotic dancing and seduction, then gathering pillow talk

FATE: Tried, sentenced to death and shot by a firing squad

LEGACY: The archetype of the glamorous, seductive female spy portrayed in novels and on screen ever since

Above: German troops on the front line. When the French divisions attacking in Champagne mutinied in May 1917, it was the moment for them to attack.

Previous page: Mata Hari, a Dutch exotic dancer and courtesan, began spying after the German Consul in The Hague offered her cash for any information she could gather on her next visit to France.

schools, and over-generous presents. Then disaster struck, and within two years she was sent to live with her godfather, in a small town called Sneek. She was not welcome there, and her next stop was a college for teachers in Leyde, whose principal, Heer Wybrandus Haanstra, an overweight disciplinarian, flirted with her too conspicuously for comfort, causing a scandal; in the custom of the times, it was M'greet who had to leave in disgrace.

Next she lodged with an uncle in The Hague, paying for her keep by doing domestic chores, until she saw a newspaper advertisement: 'Officer home from leave in the Dutch East Indies would like to meet a girl of pleasant character – object matrimony.' M'greet answered, and duly married Captain Rudolf MacLeod, 39, of the Dutch Colonial Service, on 11 July 1895, and then moved to his posting in Java. An officer he may have been, but a gentleman he certainly was not. He was an alcoholic who almost certainly had venereal disease – the couple's first child is thought to have died from congenital syphilis – and he beat her, sometimes with a whip. Perhaps as an escape, M'greet became deeply involved in Indonesian culture and especially dance, and adopted the stage name 'Mata Hari' – literally, 'the eye of the day' but meaning 'sunrise'.

The two were still physically obsessed with each other, despite the abuse. Even so, it could not last: they separated, and after a fling with another officer (M'greet never could resist a man in uniform) and a brief reconciliation with MacLeod, she left her daughter behind in The Netherlands and moved on.

The MacLeods were not formally divorced until 1907 but M'greet – now calling herself 'Lady MacLeod' – is next heard of in Paris in 1903, riding a horse in a Molier's Equestrian Circus and also working as an artist's model. (Why Paris? 'I don't know,' she once told a journalist, 'I thought all women who ran away from their husbands went to Paris.') But such transient work did not pay her bills, so she drifted into the life of a courtesan, entertaining men – the richer and more powerful they were the better. Standing 5ft 10in in her bare feet, which was tall for the times, with flirtatious dark eyes, olive skin and an hour-glass figure, she had all the attributes necessary for success, except, in her own eyes, her breasts, which she thought too small; as a result, they were always covered with a beaded, metallic bra.

An essential prop in this enterprise was her metamorphosis into her 'Mata Hari' character. Isadora Duncan had paved the way with her famous interpretation of classical Greek dances, but Mata Hari followed the Indonesian approach, which mixed art, religion – and, in her case, sex; she may have called them 'sacred dances', but they always ended with Mata Hari

OFF WITH HER HEAD

NONE OF MATA Hari's family claimed her body after her death. Instead, her head was cut off, as was the practice with criminals, and taken to the Musée d'Anatomie Delmas-Orfila-Rouvière, in Paris. This museum of anatomy, founded in 1847, had assembled a bizarre collection of more than 5,000 specimens, all of them examples of 'morbid pathology' – showing the effects on the body of malformations brought about before birth or as a result of disease. The bodies of famous murderers and serial killers were also on display, since it was believed that they suffered from a morbid pathology, too – but in this case of the brain.

It seems strange company for the last remains of a woman who had been seen as a byword for sensuality and eroticism. But it is certain that she was there once: the evidence includes an eye-witness report of the arrival of her head and a written record of the event (though this disappeared during World War II). And it is equally certain that the Museum does not have Mata Hari's head now.

So what happened to it? It could simply have been mislaid, of course – perhaps when the museum moved to its present site in 1954. But this is Mata Hari, so no simple explanation will do. The rumour has it that her head was stolen by an aging admirer in the confusion of the move. Or perhaps the thief was a 'craniomaniac' – someone with an unhealthy obsession with skulls. Stranger things have happened but, whatever the truth, it seems a sad end to the story of such an effervescent woman.

naked, apart from her bra and some floating veils. Her view was, 'dance is a poem of which each movement is a word'. On another occasion, though she was perhaps more honest: 'I could never dance well. People came to see me because I was the first who dared to show myself naked to the public.'

The French novelist Colette, author of *Gigi*, agreed: 'She didn't exactly dance; but she knew how to remove her clothes piece by piece and move her long, proud, dusky body.'

And one critic described her as: 'Feline, trembling in a thousand rhythms, exotic yet deeply austere, slender and supple like a sacred serpent.'

Whatever she did, it worked. She moved from performances in private houses to the salons of Parisian aristocracy and the stage. And as her fame grew, she danced her way round Europe, picking up titled lovers and discarding them as she went. After all, as she said: 'I am a woman who enjoys herself very much; sometimes I lose, sometimes I win.'

When World War I broke out, in August 1914, Mata Hari was stranded in Berlin, on a six-month contract to dance at the Metropol Theatre. When she tried to get out of the contract, her jewels and furs were stolen by her dresser and her bank account was frozen by the German authorities. Near destitute, she made her way back to The Netherlands, where she fell on her feet again, becoming the mistress of Baron Edouard Willem van der Capellan. But then she made a serious mistake – and it was one that was to change her life. Mata Hari was pining for the sophistication and razzmatazz of her life in Paris, so when Karl Kroemer, Honorary German Consul to The Netherlands, a neutral country, offered her 20,000 francs to spy for Germany, she accepted. Naively, she did not take him seriously, regarding the money as compensation for the theft of her property in Berlin. She threw away the invisible ink he gave her, but he recorded the transaction and gave her a codename: H-21.

In order to avoid the front line in Flanders, Mata Hari returned to Paris by way of England. En route, she was held at Folkestone by British Intelligence, who were apparently suspicious because of her looks and manner, as well as her mastery of five languages, and reported their suspicions to French Intelligence. It was also noted that she had recently been in Berlin and appeared to have money.

The French, who were worried about German spies to the point of paranoia, followed her wherever she went, questioned everybody with whom she came into contact, and steamed open her letters – without finding anything

suspicious. She had many lovers, until she met a man who was to be the love of her life: a 21-year-old Russian Captain called Vadime Masloff; he was almost half her age.

Vadime returned to the front, where he was wounded, losing an eye, and was sent to Vittel, in north-eastern France, to recuperate. Unfortunately for Mata Hari, Vittel was in the 'War Zone', so she needed a pass to visit him. The man who would sign the pass was Captain George Ladoux, the Head of French Intelligence, who was determined to prove his worth by exposing a German spy. He signed the pass, but with a condition: Mata Hari would spy on the Germans for France and be handsomely paid for doing so. Thinking that she now had a way of paying off her many debts and living happily ever after with Vadime, she agreed. Ladoux just thought, presumably, that he had acquired an expendable double agent who could further his career.

Above: St Lazaire prison, where Mata Hari was imprisoned before her trial for treason in July 1917. She was shot by firing squad at Vincennes that October.

Right: Mata Hari, Germany's spy H-21, photographed at the time of her arrest. According to the *New Yorker*, at her execution she wore 'a neat Amazonian tailored suit', specially made for the occasion.

After visiting Vadime, she tried to get back to Paris via Britain, but was arrested by British Intelligence. Ladoux intervened and she was released, but was told to go to Spain in December 1916, where she was to seduce a German Major, Arnold Kalle. Inevitably she was successful, but all she got from him was some low-level information about German activities in Morocco and the notion that French code might have been broken; she told him that the Allies were preparing a 'big push' for the Spring, but he could easily have learnt this anyway from the French newspapers.

Proudly, Mata Hari returned to France to report back to Ladoux, who refused to pay her until she provided better information. But while she was travelling, Kalle sent a report back to Berlin using a code that the French had broken (some believe that Kalle did this deliberately, just to cause consternation among the French. It referred to Mata Hari as agent H-21 of the Cologne Intelligence Section, and said that she had claimed that Britain was in military and political control of France. (According to German documents unsealed in the 1970s, she may also have given the Germans the names of six French spies at around this time.)

The French were not impressed. Mata Hari was arrested on 13 February 1917 and committed to trial. From the start, the odds were against her: the trial was held in secret; her judge and jury were all military officers. Mata Hari was represented by Edouard Clunet, a 74-year-old ex-lover whose speciality was corporate law and who had not addressed a court for years. That scarcely mattered, however, because Clunet was not allowed to question either the prosecution's witnesses or his own. Inevitably, even though the evidence against his client was negligible, the jury's verdict was guilty and the sentence was death.

And so, on 15 October 1917, Mata Hari was woken in her cell at the Prison de Sainte-Lazare at 5am and driven to a clearing in the woods outside Paris. There she faced a firing squad of 12 French colonial troops wearing fezzes. She refused a blindfold, and according to one account, blew the soldiers a kiss; in another, her last words were: 'A courtesan yes, but a traitor, never.' The rifles rang out, she slumped and an officer administered the *coup de grâce*. A sergeant-major said: 'By God, this lady knows how to die.'

So was Mata Hari a double agent or wasn't she? We will not have to wait long to find out. In 2017, the official French papers relating to the case, which were sealed for 100 years after the trial, are to be released.

Sir Roger Casement

To some he was a freedom fighter, to others a terrorist – but his attempt to free his country from foreign rule was ended by an executioner's noose

FOR A MAN who came to have an international reputation, Roger Casement's upbringing was relatively humble. He was born in 1864 to a Protestant father, a Captain of Dragoons in the British Army, and a Catholic mother, about whom little is known. His father may well have influenced Casement's adult philosophy, because he volunteered to fight in the Hungarian Revolution on 1848 – one of the wave of nationalist, pro-democracy, anti-monarchy revolutions that swept much of the world in that year. His mother almost certainly influenced him, too: she had him secretly baptized into the Catholic faith at the age of three.

Casement's mother died when he was nine and his father when he was 13. At the age of 16, in 1880, he abandoned his education – at the Diocesan School, Ballymena – to work as a clerk at a shipping company. Little is known of him from then until the 1890s, when he joined the British

FACT FILE

BORN: 1 September 1864, Kingstown, now Dun Laoghaire, County Dublin, Ireland as Roger David Casement (Ruairí Dáithí Mac Easmainn in Irish)

DIED: 3 August 1916 at Pentonville Prison, London

MISSION: To remove the British from Ireland and restore the country to Home Rule

INTELLIGENCE TECHNIQUES: Attempted to form an 'Irish Brigade' to fight the British, made up of Irish POWs in German hands, and to supply German arms to the Irish rebels

FATE: The Irish Brigade plan came to nothing and the ship carrying the arms sank. Through bad luck and the activities of British Naval Intelligence, he was captured a few days before the unsuccessful Easter Rising in Dublin, taken to England, tried and, after a failed appeal, executed by hanging

LEGACY: Still honoured and revered by many in Ireland as a patriot, freedom fighter and martyr

Consular Service, in which he rose to become British Consul in part of the French Congo, in Central Africa, in 1901.

By 1903, the Congo Free State had been run as a personal fiefdom by King Leopold II of Belgium for some 17 years. It had become a byword for tyranny, cruelty and barbarism. Casement was asked by the British government to investigate the situation and report on any human rights abuses. He did so, and in 1904 *The Casement Report* was published: it described how Leopold's troops and agents were systematically abusing the local inhabitants in the most cruel and grotesque way in order to maximize the production of rubber and other materials – all to enrich the king's personal wealth.

Following an international outcry, and the formation by Casement and others of the Congo Reform Association, Leopold was forced to cede control of the Congo Free State to the Belgian Parliament in 1908. Casement was rewarded with the CMG – the Order of St Michael and St George – by a grateful British government in 1905, and dubbed 'Congo Casement' by the British Press.

*Above :*Irish Nationalist Sir Roger Casement distinguished himself in the British Consular Service before retiring through ill-health in 1911; three years later, he helped to found the Irish National Volunteers.

In 1906, Casement was despatched to Brazil and promoted to Consul-General. He led an investigation into the working practices of the Peruvian Amazon Company, which produced rubber in Peru. Again, he exposed extraordinarily cruel treatment of workers – including the imprisonment, flogging and the forced starvation of whole families – in his 1911 report to the British government, which duly honoured him with a knighthood in the same year. But he also kept diaries of his years in Peru – something that was to come back to haunt him just five years later.

So in 1911, Sir Roger Casement seemed the model of a British gentleman, colonial officer, member of the Establishment and champion of those suffering from abuse at the hands of exploiters. But Casement applied his principles without fear or favour and had done so for many years. For him, the British were exploiters in Ireland, and his fellow countrymen were being exploited by Imperialist aggressors.

Below: A deliberately mutilated rubber worker's injuries are caught on camera. Casement won an international reputation – and his knighthood – for exposing such atrocities in the Belgian Congo and the Amazon Valley.

As early as 1904, he had joined the Gaelic League, which aimed to preserve the Irish language, and a year later he joined the recently founded Sinn Féin party, which demanded independence for Ireland. He summed up his thinking in an emotive and eloquent speech from the dock at his trial in 1916:

'Self-government is our right, a thing born to us at birth. A thing no more to be doled out to us by another people than the right to life itself; than the right to feel the sun or smell the flowers or to love our kind.'

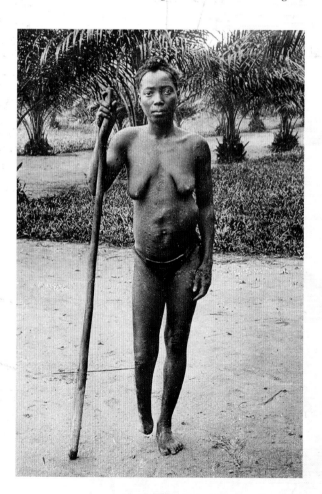

Having left Britain's Consular Service after his report on Peru, Casement was able to devote more time to the cause of Home Rule. In 1913, he helped to found the Irish Volunteers, along with Eoin MacNeill, and also helped write its manifesto: this laid the groundwork for a military organization, but one that was primarily defensive – the Ulster Volunteers had been founded the year before.

Events were now gathering a momentum of their own. It seemed likely that there would soon be a war with Germany, which was something that Casement would welcome, since a weakened, distracted Britain would be less

effective in denying Irish independence. In July 1914, he travelled to America, to meet with members of the Irish-exile organization Clan na Gael and raise money for his volunteers at home. While he was in the USA a shipment of guns from Germany was landed at Howth Harbour, near Dublin, in a blaze of publicity. Just after an unsuccessful bid to seize them, British troops killed four local civilians, pouring fuel on the flames, and outraging the Irish. (Casement had helped finance the purchase of the guns, many of which, though outdated, were used in the Easter Rising; their purchase was a response to the earlier delivery of better weapons, also from Germany, to the Ulster Volunteers at Larne, in the north of Ireland.)

Casement was still in New York when World War I started in August 1914. His response was to hold meetings with German diplomats, offering to

Above: Linenhall Barracks on Constitution Hill in Dublin was deliberately set on fire by rebel Irish Nationalists during the Easter Rising to try to prevent them being reoccupied by the British.

Above: German submarines at Kiel harbour in 1914. The two in the centre of the front row, U20 and U19, would carry Casement back to Ireland from Germany.

arrange an Irish rebellion to divert British troops in return for money and arms. The meetings were inconclusive, so Casement decided to present his case in person and travelled to Germany via Norway – from there, the British Ambassador reported back to London what Casement was up to; his information also gave the British government its first inkling that Casement might be homosexual *(see box)*.

In Germany, Casement continued his negotiations for arms, and also tried to raise an 'Irish Brigade' of Irish prisoners-of-war who had been serving in the British Army. His attempts were unsuccessful, and only 56 of a possible 2,200 men joined up – many of them purely because they were near starvation. Nothing was to come of the Irish Brigade. Casement was also disappointed by the German response to his request for arms: all they were prepared to give him were 20,000 old rifles, ten machine guns and some ammunition. Nevertheless, this consignment was loaded onto a cargo ship called the *Libau* – though it was disguised as a Norwegian boat called the *Aud-Norge* – which duly set sail for Ireland.

BLACK AND WHITE

EVEN AFTER BEING found guilty of treason, Casement was still held in considerable regard by many of the great and the good, mainly as a result of his previous work in the Congo and Peru. The death sentence he received was thought by many to be far too harsh and pressure for a reprieve started to grow; it was led by literati such as Sir Arthur Conan Doyle, creator of Sherlock Holmes, and George Bernard Shaw, the Anglo-Irish playwright.

The British had already executed many of the leaders of the Easter Rising, and were in no mood for clemency. They handed the task of stifling the opposition to Admiral Sir Reginald 'Blinker' Hall, the notoriously ruthless Head of Naval Intelligence, whose radio-intercept offices had been responsible for catching Casement in the first place. His solution was to discreetly circulate extracts from Casement's diaries among them – or, at least, what he claimed were Casement's diaries, as we shall see.

Above: Rear Admiral Sir Reginald Hall was instrumental in the establishment of Room 40, the Royal Navy codebreaking operation. Room 40 was responsible for the interception of the *Libau/Aud-Norge*.

Casement had, apparently, kept diaries all his life, but they were diaries with a difference: one set was innocent – 'the White Diaries'; the other was far from it. The first contained detailed, but run-of-the-mill accounts of his daily life and work. But in the 'Black Diaries' was a no-holds-barred record of numerous homosexual encounters. The English poet Alfred Noyes wrote: 'I have seen and read them and they touch the lowest depths that human degradation has ever touched. Page after page of his diary would be an insult to a pig's trough to let the foul record touch it.'

Judged by the morality of the time, this was a killer blow. The call for a reprieve died down swiftly and Hall and the British government had won: Casement's appeal failed and his sentence was duly carried out. But were the Black Diaries genuine?

Controversy has raged ever since. For decades, the British government hardly helped its cause by denying that the diaries had ever existed. They were released only in 1959, and most experts thought that they were genuine. Even so, some in Ireland found it impossible to believe that an Irish Nationalist could be gay – nobody had ever suspected this of Casement when he was alive. Others pointed to discrepancies between the two versions of events for the same day. Yet more claimed that the Black Diaries had been Casement's transcriptions, for evidential purposes, of the diaries of one Armondo Normand, a Peruvian who was famously cruel – but also a voracious and predatory heterosexual.

A Symposium was held in Dublin in 2000 to attempt to resolve the matter. It recommended that the diaries should be examined forensically, and in 2002 Dr Audrey Giles, an internationally renowned handwriting expert, presented her verdict: 'The writings throughout the documents show many similarities to the writings of Roger Casement and no significant differences.'

Case over? Probably not. Critics point out that only the handwriting was tested, not the paper, ink, pollen residues and so on. And in the 1980s, the 'Hitler Diaries' were bought by the *Times* of London having been validated by three handwriting experts before being shown to be forgeries.

Time will tell. But Casement was still hanged.

Right: After being apprehended at Tralee Bay, Casement was taken to the foreboding Tower of London, a castle which has held political prisoners for eight centuries, to await his treason trial.

Casement knew that this quantity of arms was insufficient to sustain the Easter Rising, planned for late April 1916, and tried to send a message to the Irish Volunteers so that it could be postponed. The message never got through. He, meanwhile, was travelling back to Ireland on a German submarine, the SM *U-20*. This developed engine trouble, so he had to re-embark on another submarine, the SM *U19*.

The *Libau/Aud-Norge* was intercepted by HMS *Bluebell*, a British warship, as it neared Ireland – as a result of communications interceptions by British Naval Intelligence – and was scuttled by its crew as it approached harbour on 22 April; the German arms were now at the bottom of the sea. The day before, Casement had landed at Tralee Bay, County Kerry and promptly been arrested. In short order, he was charged with treason, spying and sabotage and dispatched to England and the Tower of London.

Three days later, the Easter Rising began in Dublin. The Irish fighters were massively outnumbered and also under-armed; the rising lasted for just six days before petering out. Around 1,500 Irish fighters were interned and 15 of the leaders were executed – one of them, James Connolly, while tied to a chair because a broken ankle prevented him from standing.

It was clear to all at Casement's trial that he had colluded with Britain's enemy. But was that treason? The problem for the prosecution – one of whom was Sir George Branson, Sir Richard Branson's grandfather – was that treason was defined in the Treason Act of 1371 as something involving offences against 'the King in his Realm' and 'giving to them [his enemies] Aid and Comfort in the Realm or elsewhere'. This, Casement's counsel argued, meant that 'elsewhere' applied to the giving of aid and comfort, which he had not done. The prosecution argued that 'elsewhere' applied to the Realm and extended the jurisdiction of the Act. The judges found that there was a mark on the ancient parchment that might indicate a comma. So Casement was found guilty and sentenced to death.

By the account of John Ellis, the executioner, Sir Roger Casement met his death bravely and with dignity. He had been confirmed in the Catholic faith in the condemned cell, and from it he wrote in a letter:

'It is a strange, strange fate, and now, as I stand face to face with death I feel just as if they were going to kill a boy. For I feel like a boy – and my hands so free from blood, and my heart always so compassionate and pitiful, that I cannot comprehend how anyone wants to hang me.'

Left: The memorial to Sir Roger Casement was erected near the spot where he disembarked from a German U-boat on April 21 1916. He met his end at Pentonville Prison, London, on August 3, 1916.

BETRAYED BY THE COUNTRY HE SAVED

Richard Sorge

He was arguably the most influential spy for any of the fighting in World War II. Without him Hitler might well have defeated Stalin and the world would have been very different today

ON THE MORNING of Tuesday 7 November 1944, at 10:20am, the man whose intelligence had saved the Soviet Union in its war against Nazi Germany was taken from his cell in the Sugamo Prison, Tokyo and hanged. It was three years since he had first been sentenced to death by the Japanese for spying, and on three occasions – according to General Tominaga, Chief of Staff of the Japanese army in Manchuria (Northeast China), speaking after the war – he had been offered to the Soviets as an exchange prisoner. On each occasion, the Soviets denied any knowledge of him. Richard Sorge had been left to his fate.

Sorge was born in Azerbaijan in 1895, the son of a German mining engineer and a Russian mother; tellingly, he was the great-nephew of Friedrich Adolf Sorge, an associate of Marx and Engels. In 1898, Sorge's family moved back to Germany, but his well-to-do household maintained its Russian influences. Even so, when World War I started in August 1914, Sorge enlisted

FACT FILE

BORN: 4 October 1895, Baku, Azerbaijan
DIED: 7 November 1944, in the Sugamo Prison, Tokyo
MISSION: To further the cause of the Soviet Union and communism and help defeat its enemies
INTELLIGENCE TECHNIQUES: working undercover as a journalist, cultivating government and military sources with the help of a ring of agents; reporting back by means of radio and one-time code pads
FATE: Tried, sentenced to death, offered three times to The Soviet Union in a prisoner exchange; disavowed by the Soviets and so hanged
LEGACY: A reputation as perhaps the most influential spy of World War II and recognized as such by the Soviets after Stalin's death, when he was honoured in memorials, on stamps and in books and films

Above: German artillery on the French front in 1916. Sorge served in a unit much like this until he was invalided out of the army.

in a student battalion of the German Army's 3rd Guards Field Artillery in the German Army. He was badly wounded on the Western Front in 1916, losing three fingers to shrapnel and having his legs shattered (he walked with a limp for the rest of his life), and was medically discharged. Nevertheless, he had served with distinction and was promoted to corporal and awarded the (Iron Cross Second Class) – something that was to serve him well in his later activities.

While recuperating from his wounds, Sorge seduced a nurse – seduction is a theme that runs through his life, as does heavy drinking – whose Marxist father taught him the basis of communism. He took this interest further at university, where he studied economics and political science, gaining a PhD, and joined the German Communist Party in 1919.

Sorge thrived in the post-war years of Germany's Weimar Republic; he was young, handsome, charismatic, a decorated war hero, driven by his plans for a new world order and, it seems, irresistible to women. In 1922 he married Christine Gerlach, having charmed her husband, a Communist

professor who had taught Sorge, into granting her an amicable divorce. Christine described Sorge as 'something dangerous, dark, inescapable'.

Having worked as a journalist and having also helped to establish a Marxist think-tank, Sorge moved to Moscow in 1924; some accounts suggest that he was in trouble with the police in Germany. It was a bid to live his life in what he considered to be the brave new world. Soon he had joined the International Liaison Department of the Comintern (the 'Communist International', an intelligence gathering operation) and also the Red Army's Fourth Department, which was to become the military intelligence outfit GRU – this workload, or perhaps his chronic infidelity, led to his divorce.

After the Soviets had taught him about 'tradecraft', Sorge was activated as an agent and started to travel the world, developing contacts and building up spy networks – always working undercover, mainly as a journalist. In 1929, he was in Britain, assessing its Communist Party and the country's politics. Later that year, he returned to Germany, where, on Comintern instructions, he joined the Nazi Party.

In 1930, he was sent to China, where tensions between Japan and China were reaching boiling point over the territory of Manchuria (Northeast China). He reported on the eventual fighting and Japanese military capabilities, became an expert on Chinese agriculture, and also met various agents, all Communists, who would be of great use to him in the future: Max Klausen (though German, a Red Army officer and radio operator), Agnes Smedley (a noted American journalist, who was also his lover) and, through her, Hotsumi Ozaki, a Japanese journalist. He also gained another wife: Yekaterina 'Katya' Maximova, a drama student.

Japan's military success in Manchuria made the Soviets fearful of its expansionary plans: would it strike – if so, would it be north, to Russia

THE AMERICAN CONNECTION

DURING WORLD WAR II, Moscow's spies were motivated by a political philosophy that knew no boundaries, rather than by patriotism and, as a result, found it easy to slot into the Comintern's espionage network anywhere in the world. This became clear when Japanese Government Prosecutor Mitsusada Yoshikawa started to investigate rumours of a spy ring in Tokyo in Japan in 1941.

After receiving a vague tip-off, Yoshikawa started to investigate Yotoku Miyagi, a Japanese-born artist who had left his native Okinawa to join his father in America, where he had travelled to look for work. He had already been primed with socialist principles by his grandfather in Japan, and in 1927 a radical organization he had founded joined up with the American Communist Party. (He may have met Richard Sorge during a trip he made to America before World War II, at which Sorge is known to have met at least one Soviet agent.)

By 1932, the Comintern in Moscow had asked Sorge to set up a spy ring in Japan – but Sorge spoke no Japanese. Miyagi, however, spoke both Japanese and English and, just as important, was a Communist. On Moscow's instructions, he answered a classified advertisement in a Los Angeles newspaper and before long he was in contact with, first, Branko Vukelić and then Richard Sorge – he was soon installed in Tokyo as Sorge's invaluable assistant.

Under Yoshikawa's none-too-gentle interrogation, Miyagi broke down and tried to commit suicide by jumping out of a window. Yoshikawa's men pulled him back and asked him to explain why a top-secret document had been found at his house. The game was up: Sorge's spy ring was wound up and Miyagi died in prison during his trial – he was awarded The Order of the Great Patriotic War (Second Class) by the Soviets in 1964.

Much of Miyagi's story came out in August 1951, in Yashikawa's testimony at the US House of Representatives Committee of Un-American Activities hearings into Sorge's spy ring, and its implication for US security during the Cold War. The Committee's goal, in those days of paranoia about 'reds under the bed', was to find evidence to implicate a noted American journalist and writer called Agnes Smedley in spying; she had also become famous through publications such as *Daughter of the Earth* (1933) and *China's Red Army Marches* (1934).

Smedley had been Sorge's lover in China in the 1930s and was a lifelong Communist and activist. Sorge incriminated her during his confession, but she was nevertheless defended by a number of Washington politicians. However, we will never know the full truth about what influence she and other members of Sorge's ring in America had: she died in a nursing home in Britain in 1950. But, Smedley, too, might well have been one of the 'reds under the bed' so feared by the US.

Right: This young conscript was one of the hundreds and thousands who served in Japan's so-called Kwantung army as, having conquered Manchuria, it drove further into China and Mongolia.

(it was only 25 years since the two countries had fought a war) or south? To find out, the Comintern ordered Sorge to set up a spy ring in Japan.

First, Sorge had to obtain journalistic credentials. He returned to Berlin, where as an Iron Cross holder and member of the Nazi Party he was welcomed in the Nazi beer halls – even though he had given up drink completely to avoid letting anything slip. Before long, he had letters of accreditation from several newspapers who would publish his dispatches from Japan. Travelling to Japan by way of America, where he had several meetings with American Communists, he arrived there in September 1933 – reporting back to Moscow using the codename 'Рамзай', or 'Ramsay'.

Sorge's spy ring was soon established. It included two old friends, Max Klausen and Hotsumi Osaki, as well as Branko Vukelić, a journalist working for a French newspaper, Shigeru Mizuno, a student agitator and Yotokti Miyagi, a Japanese artist who had joined the Communist Party in America – and would bring about Sorge's downfall. Over the next few years, more agents were enlisted, to form a truly international network.

The work that Sorge had put in to developing his contacts and cover stories over the years now started to bear fruit. As a Nazi and decorated war veteran he was made welcome at the German Embassy, where he made a friend of the Ambassador, Herbert von Dirkson and the Military Attache, Colonel Eugen Ott – he even bedded Ott's wife Helma, apparently with Ott's knowledge. In fact, his enduring reputation as a rampant seducer and heavy drinker made it hard for anybody to believe it possible that he was a spy. Sorge was able to send a wealth of information back to Moscow, such as the state of negotiations between Germany and Japan to establish the 'Anti-Comintern Pact'.

Two items of intelligence stand out – not least because they almost certainly changed the political and military map of the world. In 1941, Hitler turned his attention away from Britain and towards the Soviet Union, his ally at the time. Sorge discovered from Ott, who was now the Ambassador, that some 180 German divisions were in place on the Soviet border, ready to invade, and Stalin was warned in a radio message on 1 June. Stalin – who was already aware of the Anti-Comintern Pact, dismissed the warning as a 'provocation.' On 21 June, Sorge tried again, warning that the invasion would take place within days. Again his warning was dismissed. On 22 June, Germany invaded the Soviet Union.

Within a short time, the situation became desperate for the Soviets. But Hotsumi Osaki had become a close friend of the Japanese Prime Minster, Prince Fumimaro Konoe, and even an adviser to him. Osaki was able to report that Japan intended to expand, but to the south, where it would fight America and Britain. Japan, Sorge was able to report to Moscow in September, would not attack Russia unless Moscow had fallen and the Japanese troops had a numerical advantage in their area of attack of three to one.

Right: Japan and Nazi Germany concluded their Anti-Comintern Pact in 1936 (a copy of the signed treaty is seen here). Sorge kept Moscow informed of each stage of the negotiations.

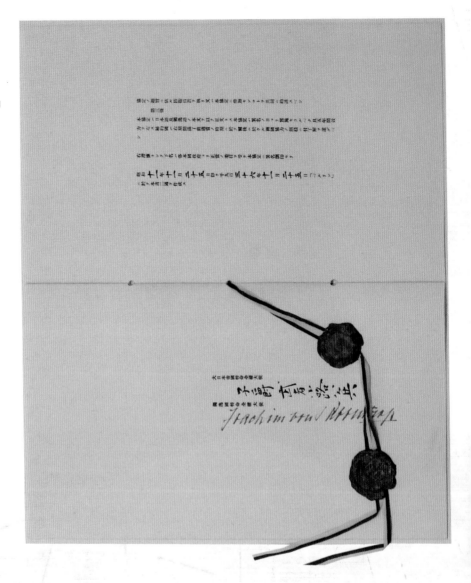

As a direct result of this information, Stalin was able to move 18 divisions, 1,700 tanks and 1,500 aircraft back from the Far East to Moscow, where they proved decisive in the battle for the city between October 1941 and January 1942 and helped inflict the first defeat of the war on Hitler: the tide had turned.

Meanwhile, the Japanese attacked the Americans at Pearl Harbour, on 7 December 1941. Stalin had failed to pass on Sorge's earlier warning. In mid-October,1941, Sorge's network was rolled up by the Japanese. Yotokti

Miyagi had been arrested after a tip-off and revealed all after a brutal interrogation. Sorge, Osaki, Vukelić and Klausen were all rounded up, and sufficient incriminating evidence was found on them to make anything but a confession impossible. Vukelić and Klausen were sentenced to life imprisonment, while Sorge and Osaki were sentenced to death.

Sorge was offered back to Moscow in exchange for a Japanese prisoner on three occasions, but on each one the Soviets denied any knowledge of him. In fact, Stalin was so embarrassed by his failure to take Sorge's warnings about the German invasion seriously that he wanted nothing to do with him – so he and Osaki were hanged in 1944. Yet he did have Sorge's wife Katya arrested: charged, ludicrously, with being a German spy, she was sent to a labour camp in Siberia, where she died.

It was a grave disservice to a loyal Soviet operative. Richard Sorge had remained a true and proud Communist to the last. Giving testimony to a hearing of the US House of Representatives Committee on Un-American Activities into US nationals' involvement in the Sorge spy ring, in August 1951, Japanese prosecutor Mitsusado Yashikawa revealed what Sorge had said in his confession: 'I have been an international Communist since 1925 and I am still ... I have never been defeated since I became an international Communist. This is the first time that I was beaten.'

After Stalin's death in 1953, Sorge's work was re-evaluated. Suddenly he was made a 'Hero of The Soviet Union' and awarded the Order of Lenin; his face appeared on a postage stamp in 1965 and a monument to him stands at Khimki, outside Moscow – the closest to Moscow that the German troops reached. Richard Sorge would no doubt have preferred that the Soviets had acknowledged his existence some ten years earlier.

Even Sorge's enemies could not fail to acknowledge the significance of what he had done or the skill with which he had done it. US Army General Douglas MacArthur described his activities as, 'A devastating example of a brilliant success of espionage'.

Perhaps the greatest accolade came from journalist, novelist and author of *The Day of the Jackal*, Frederick Forsyth

'The spies in history who can say from their graves, the information I supplied to my masters, for better or worse, altered the history of our planet, can be counted on the fingers of one hand. Richard Sorge was in that group.'

Special Operations Executive

From 1940 onwards, dedicated secret agents and saboteurs fulfilled Winston Churchill's dramatic directive – to set Nazi-occupied Europe ablaze. They were the British premier's Secret Army

IN JULY 1940, with Britain and its Commonwealth standing alone against the might of the Third Reich, the indomitable Winston Churchill, firmly established in the saddle having replaced Neville Chamberlain as the country's Prime Minister two months earlier, was determined to strike back. He told Hugh Dalton, previously a prominent leader of the Labour Opposition whom he now appointed Minister of Economic Warfare, that he was putting him in charge of a new subversive operation as well. Its task, Churchill somewhat grandiloquently stated, was to 'set Europe ablaze'.

The Special Operations Executive – SOE for short – had been born, though, perhaps surprisingly, the original idea for

FACT FILE

FOUNDED: 16 July 1940
DISBANDED: 15 January 1946
MISSION: Aiding local resistance movements, raiding operations, special reconnaissance and sabotage in Europe, Scandinavia and Southeast Asia
INTELLIGENCE TECHNIQUES: Fake identities, disguise, codes, assassination, clandestine wireless transmissions, sabotage
FATE: Officially disbanded after the war; unofficially 280 staff became part of SIS, the Secret Intelligence Service MI6
LEGACY: SOE was the model for its US counterpart – the Office of Strategic Services (OSS), which evolved into the Central Intelligence Service (CIA)

it came from Chamberlain and not from Churchill at all. Dalton further defined its purpose. 'It was to coordinate all action by way of subversion and sabotage against the enemy overseas', he wrote in his post-war memoirs, *The Fatal Years*. Its beginnings were small – it started by absorbing the Secret Intelligence Service's D Section, which had been set up in April 1938 – but, as Dalton recorded, it swiftly grew.

What resulted, Dalton went on to note, 'would be a secret or underground organization. There would be no public announcement of my new responsibility, and knowledge of its activities would be kept within a very restricted circle. As to its scope, "sabotage" was a simple idea. It meant smashing things up. "Subversion" was a more complex conception. It meant the weakening, by whatever covert means, of the enemy's will and power to make war, and the strengthening of the will and power of his opponents, including in particular guerrilla and resistance movements.' SOE would wage, Dalton concluded with some relish, 'an ungentlemanly war'.

Above: Captain Adolphe Rabinovich was parachuted twice into France by SOE. The second time on 3 March 1944 the Germans were waiting; he was taken to Gross Rosen concentration camp and executed with 17 SOE comrades.

SOE started life in offices in Caxton Street, London, but these quickly became too small to hold the burgeoning organization. In October 1940, its headquarters moved to 64 Baker Street; SOE eventually expanded to occupy six more large buildings in the vicinity. The chosen cover name was the Inter-Services Research Bureau. Because of Baker Street's close association with Sir Arthur Conan Doyle's fictional detective Sherlock Holmes, it was small wonder that SOE's operatives earned themselves the nickname of 'the Baker Street Irregulars.'

That was only the London end of the operation. As time passed, SOE spread its tentacles wider and wider. In the end, there were around 60 training schools in Britain with more overseas. In out-of-the-way locations that stretched from the Highlands to the New Forest, would-be operatives were taught how to kill with their bare hands; how to

Above: Codenamed Rose, Eileen Nearne was an SOE courier and wireless operator in Paris after parachuting into France just days before her 23rd birthday in March 1944; she was captured but escaped in 1945.

disguise themselves; how to derail a train; and even how to get out of a pair of handcuffs with the aid of a piece of thin wire and a diary pencil

Two of the most colourful characters in SOE – William Ewart Fairburn and Eric Anthony 'Bill' Sykes – taught unarmed combat, fast shooting and the skills of silent killing. Major Henry Hall of the Dorset Regiment recalled his first encounter with them when he was posted to Inverailort House in the western Highlands in February 1941 for guerrilla warfare training. 'We gathered at the foot of a large staircase,' he later recalled, 'and two old gentlemen, aged approximately 58 and 56, dressed in battledress with the rank of captain and both wearing glasses, appeared at the top of the stairs and proceeded to fall down the stairs together and landed in a battle crouch position with a handgun in one hand and a Fairburn-Sykes knife in the other.'

Hall soon realized that the 'heavenly twins,' as Sykes and Fairburn were dubbed within SOE, were anything but heavenly. They were both ruthless to the core. Indeed, it was Sykes who trained the Czech operatives despatched to assassinate Reinhardt Heydrich, the Reichsprotektor of Bohemia and deputy head of the SS, in Prague in 1942. The wireless transmission the operatives sent to confirm that they had landed safely ended: 'Give Bill Sykes our best wishes – tell him we won't miss.'

To give operatives a further edge, backroom boys busied themselves devising special weapons. At The Frythe, a secluded mansion near Welwyn Garden City, Hertfordshire, SOE technical wizards devised such ingenious gadgets as the single-shot cigarette pistol and the so-called Sleeping Beauty, a submersible canoe. They also developed carborundum. This was an abrasive paste which, when smeared over the right place, could bring a railway locomotive to an immediate halt. A roadhouse called 'The Thatched Barn' in north London became the headquarters of SOE's camouflage section. Supervised by one-time film director Elder Wills, an army of former prop makers were put to work creating countless illusions out of papier maché and plaster. A carefully-modelled fake tree trunk, for instance, could be used as a hiding place for a radio transmitter; what looked like camel dung was a booby trap, consisting of enough plastic explosives to blow the wheels off a passing enemy truck. The 'time pencils' used to detonate such explosives were yet another SOE invention.

Above: A still from a US Navy training film shows the 'Sleeping Beauty' canoe – officially the Motorized Submersible Canoe – one of the technological gadgets supplied to SOE operatives for use in Europe and the Far East.

Nothing was left to chance. Even the clothes the operatives wore were specially tailored to look like the genuine article. Claudia Pulver, a seamstress who had been trained as a fashion designer before the war, specialized in styling fake clothing. Everything down to the labels had to look genuine enough to escape detection. Bert Adlington was the 'ager'; his job was to make clothing look worn, rather than brand new.

Agents who were selected to become wireless operators underwent protracted and demanding training. They learned to encode messages in

ASSASSINATING HITLER

IN LATE 1944, SOE operatives prepared to launch one of their boldest operations yet – the assassination of Adolf Hitler, Germany's faltering Fuehrer. Their plot, codenamed Operation Foxley, was ingenious to say the least, though, even today, the identity of the agent who headed its planning remains a secret. Officially, he only exists as a codename – Agent LB/X.

The planners had a wealth of information to draw on, some of which came from a former member of Hitler's bodyguard who had been captured in Normandy. Various schemes were proposed, the most far-fetched of which was to poison the water supply on Hitler's special train while it was drawn up in the sidings at Salzburg station. Eventually, it was decided that the best option was for a sniper to try to assassinate the Fuehrer when he took his customary morning walk from the Berghof, his home in the Bavarian Alps, to the nearby Teahouse. He practically always walked there on his own, though his SS bodyguards followed at a discreet distance.

The plan, though ingenious, was never put into effect. It was feared that a dead Fuehrer would become a martyr, while many Allied commanders in the field argued that, because of the strategic blunders he was likely to commit, a live Hitler was of more use to them than a dead one.

Above: This SOE insignia sums up what the organization was all about – as Prime Minister Winston Churchill instructed, its mission was to 'set Europe ablaze'.

cipher and to transmit them in Morse at a rate of at least 22 characters a minute. Operators were given their own individual codes; they were also encouraged to develop their own 'fist', or transmitting style, so that whoever was receiving their messages could tell who was sending them. They also had to learn how to fix problems and repair faults when things went wrong with their radio sets.

Most SOE wireless operators were trained in special schools like Thame Park in Oxfordshire. Parachutists learned to parachute at Ringway airfield near Manchester, dropping out of their aircraft over Tatton Park, where they were billeted. All prospective operators spent their last few weeks of their training at so-called Finishing Schools, such as the one at Beaulieu in Hampshire's New Forest. There, they were tested and retested on the cover stories they had been given over and over again to make sure they were word perfect in every detail.

The final test was the most daunting of all. In the early hours of the morning, would-be operatives were roused from their slumber and hauled down into the cellars to be subjected to mock interrogations carried out by men dressed in Gestapo uniform. The treatment was harsh, but it was a necessary preparation to increase the chances of survival if confronted with the real thing in the field.

It began on 5 May 1941, when Georges Bégué, the son of a French engineer who had volunteered to fight on with the British Army after the fall of France became the first SOE operative to be parachuted into France. He was a trained wireless operator and the purpose of his mission was to establish radio communication between London, the French Resistance and the first of the various circuits of agents SOE planned to establish throughout the country.

The mission did not get off to a particularly auspicious start. Not only was Bégué dropped off target, but his parachute cords got tangled as he descended, causing him to spin round and round in mid-air. Someone had forgotten to check that bread and meat coupons were attached to his fake ration card, while Frédéric, the code name for Max Hymans, his contact in the Indre area of the Loire valley just inside the Unoccupied Zone of France, had not been forewarned of his arrival. When the two men managed to make contact, Hymans interrogated Bégué for five hours before accepting that he was a genuine SOE operative and not a German agent provocateur.

Once his credentials were accepted, Bégué set to work. Two more operatives were swiftly parachuted in to join him and, on 13 June, SOE dropped its first consignment of arms to them. At the beginning of August, two more operatives arrived, followed by another six and then one more. The risk, however, grew with each new arrival. The Germans started intercepting Bégué's transmission, though they were unable to pinpoint their place of origin.

As enemy surveillance became more and more intense, Bégué moved to Limoges and then to Perigueux, where he was shocked to see two of his fellow operatives being led in handcuffs out of the train station. He then made for Carcassonne and then for Marseilles, where the Vichy security services finally caught and arrested him. After a prolonged interrogation, during which he managed to convince his captors that he was not the mystery wireless operator they were seeking but merely an assistant, he was imprisoned – first at Beleyeme and then at Mauzac on the Dordogne about 15 miles upstream from Bergerac. It was from there that he and two other operatives managed to escape with the aid of two friendly guards – first to Lyon and then to neutral Spain via Perpignan. He was eventually repatriated to London in October 1942.

Coincidentally, it was also in May 1941 when SOE sent its first female operative into France. She was Gillian Gerson, a young actress from South America who had recently married a Frenchman. Because she had retained Chilean nationality, she could travel as a neutral to Vichy France. She spent a couple of months there before returning to Britain via Spain, loaded with useful information. In the same month that Gerson left for France, Virginia Hall, an American journalist, began a crash SOE training

Above: Virginia Hall, a redoubtable American journalist who had a wooden leg, was one of the first SOE operatives to work in Vichy France, using the cover of being a neutral to cloak her real activities.

course in readiness for her first mission to France at the end of August. As a neutral, she travelled openly to Vichy and then to Lyon, which she made her base as she started organizing what became known to SOE as the HECKLER circuit. Dennis Rake, one of her fellow operatives, described her as 'one of the great women agents of the war.'

Even after Germany went to war with the USA, Hall managed to continue her activities until the Germans proceeded to occupy the whole of France after the Allied landings in French North Africa in November 1942. Making her getaway from Lyon just ahead of the Gestapo, Hall managed to travel across the Pyrenees on foot into Spain. She got back to London in January 1943.

Hall asked to be sent back to France again, but SOE turned down the request. Colonel Maurice Buckmaster, the head of the French Section, felt that she was simply too well-known to the Germans to be redeployed in the field. Hall turned to the OSS, which had no such inhibitions. She was landed by a torpedo boat on the Brittany coast near Brest in March 1944, after which she remained active with the *Maquis*, the rural guerilla bands of French Resistance fighters, until France's liberation.

Right: The Violet Szabo memorial to SOE members on the Albert Embankment, London. Szabo was captured in France in June 1940, brutally interrogated, then deported to Germany and executed with three other female SOE operatives at Ravensbruck in February 1945.

Left: Five members of the *Maquis* raise the rifles they used to hold off the Nazis in Marseilles before the entry of Allied troops. Virginia Hall served with a rural guerrilla band much like this from 1944 until the end of the war.

Hall was fortunate. She survived the war. Many other SOE operatives were not as lucky. In France alone, out of the 400 to 500 operatives SOE deployed there, around 119 men were caught by the Germans. Only 17 survived captivity. Out of a total of 40 female operatives SOE sent to the country, 14 never returned. Four of them perished in the Natzweiler concentration camp, three at Dachau, four at Ravensbruck and one in Belsen. Wireless operators were particularly at risk. In mid-1943, SOE estimated that they were surviving for an average of just six weeks in the field before being forced off the air or captured.

By the time the war came to an end, SOE's reach had become global. There were overseas headquarters in Cairo, Algiers, India, Ceylon (present-day Sri Lanka) and Australia. At its peak, some 10,000 men and 3,000 women worked for it, aiding, in Europe alone, an estimated two to three million active resistance members. Even today, its archives continue to yield up almost unbelievable tales of courage and audacity.

The Hunt for the Red Orchestra

With tentacles stretching from France, Belgium and Holland to neutral Sweden and penetrating into the innermost levels of the German High Command, it took German counterintelligence two years to bring the leaders of this Soviet spy ring to account

FACT FILE

FOUNDED: Began operating in 1939

DISBANDED: Largely deactivated in 1942 but Swiss agent still operating in 1944 until his arrest

MISSION: To pass secrets about German military intentions, mainly on the Eastern Front, and the state of the war effort to the GRU (Soviet Military Intelligence). Operated in France, Belgium, the Netherlands, Germany, Switzerland

INTELLIGENCE TECHNIQUES: Fake identities, codes and ciphers, clandestine wireless transmissions

FATE: Though 217 of its agents were tracked down, 143 of whom were murdered, died in concentration camps or killed themselves, the most important managed to survive

LEGACY: Considered one of the largest and most effective spy networks in the history of espionage

IT WAS THE the Nazi intelligence service, the *Abwehr*, that gave the Soviet espionage network in Western Europe its name. They christened it *Die Rote Kapelle* (the Red Orchestra). Its tentacles extended into Occupied France, Belgium, Holland, neutral Switzerland and even into the heart of the Third Reich itself. As well as Russians, its agents and informants included Polish Jews, Frenchmen, Belgians, Dutchmen, Hungarians, Swiss, Germans and at least one Englishman. Disparate though this mixed bag of nationalities might appear, they were extremely effective, in fact, one of the most successful spy rings of all time.

For German counterintelligence, the story started on 26 June 1941. Four days after Hitler launched his surprise invasion of the Soviet Union, a German radio-interception station at Kranz on the Baltic coast of East Prussia intercepted a coded message being sent by a clandestine short-wave transmitter in an unknown location. Further transmissions followed over the next four nights.

A hue and cry to locate the transmitter was soon in full swing. The messages were being sent on a frequency the Germans knew was currently being employed by the Norwegian Resistance, but it obviously was not responsible for these new transmissions. Lieutenant-Colonel Hans Kopp, commander of the *Funkabwehr* (German Signals Security), sent out an urgent order to radio-monitoring stations throughout German and Nazi-occupied Europe to track down the transmissions' source. 'Essential discover PTX (the call-sign the wireless operator was using) schedule', his order read. 'Night frequency 10,363 kilocycles. Day frequency unknown. Priority 1a.'

Above: Leopold Trepper, the Polish-born *Grand Chef* of the Red Orchestra spy ring, photographed during a newspaper interview in 1972. His task had been to lay the basis of Soviet spying activity in Western Europe.

Above: Using short-wave transmitters like the one above, the Red Orchestra's wireless operators – 'pianists' as they were termed – started communicating with Moscow in May 1940; by mid-1941, they had transmitters operating in Brussels, Berlin and Holland.

Over the next two months, a further 250 messages were intercepted, but every effort to pinpoint their source failed. The best Kopp's radio experts could suggest was that they were originating from somewhere in southern Holland, Belgium or northeastern France.

As if this was not enough for the sorely-taxed Kopp, in July the monitoring stations at Kranz and Breslau started picking up messages from a second transmitter using the same five-figure code as the first one. This time, the position of the transmitter was easier to establish. It was located less than five miles from Kopp's own headquarters in Berlin. The cryptologists analysing the signals – more than 500 had been sent by the start of September – told Kopp that, though they could not decode them, the cipher being employed was undoubtedly of Russian origin.

Gradually, as Kopp's search teams narrowed down the likely area, it became clear that the wireless operator was moving between three locations. To complicate matters further, he or she was transmitting intermittently and also constantly changing the call-sign and transmission frequencies. Then the transmissions suddenly ceased altogether. The wireless operator, it seemed, had been warned that the Germans were closing in for the kill.

The other transmitter, however, was still operating – indeed, Kopp's technicians reported it was now on the air for up to five hours at a stretch every night. By this time, too, his experts had established that the transmissions were originating in Belgium, probably from the coastal area between Ghent and Bruges. Kopp turned to the Abwehr to help him to finally locate it and Captain Harry Piepe was assigned the task. He met with no success at first until Kopp's technicians came to his aid. They discovered that the transmissions were now originating from Brussels. Piepe went undercover there, posing as a businessman with an office in the Rue Royale in the city centre.

New radio-detection vans took to the streets. Through them, the Germans found out that they were looking for three transmitters, all using the same call-signs and wavelengths, rather than one. The search was narrowed down to the Etterbeck district southeast of the city centre, the suburb of Ukkel and the Laeken district to the northeast. Rather than wait for all three transmitters to be pinpointed, however, Piepe decided to home in on the Etterbeck one first. If he could catch its operator, he reasoned, he would soon persuade him or her to reveal the exact locations of the other transmitters.

At 2.00am on 14 December 1941, Piepe and his men raided three adjoining houses in the Rue des Atrebates. They struck lucky, catching the wireless operator and two female assistants – a courier and a cipher expert – in the

LITTLE REWARD

LEOPOLD TREPPER RETURNED to Moscow in January 1945 – six years after leaving the Soviet Union to become the *Grand Chef* of the GRU spy network in Western Europe. He did not receive a hero's welcome. Despite his protestations that he had been playing a double game with his captors, Moscow Centre condemned him for having collaborated with the Germans by agreeing to transmit false information to it after his arrest in November 1942. He served nine years and seven months in the Lubianka and Lefortovo prisons before being released in May 1954. Three years later, he and his family settled in Warsaw; in 1973, he emigrated to Israel to get away from anti-Semitic persecution in his native land.

Sandor Radko, the Hungarian who headed the Red Orchestra's Swiss operation, met a similar fate. His approaches to British Intelligence in October and November 1943 and his embezzlement of GRU funds to pay for his lavish lifestyle in Geneva earned him ten years in the Lubianka and other Soviet prisons, after which he returned to his homeland.

Above: German fighting on the Eastern Front. The Red Orchestra's reports on the Wehrmacht's losses were devastating to the Reich.

act, One of them, Rita Arnould, a German Jewess and fugitive from the Gestapo, turned informant. The others refused to talk, even when the Gestapo took over their interrogation. The other members of the Belgian contingent of the Red Orchestra went to ground.

It was not until mid-1942 that the Laeken radio started transmitting again. On 30 June, Piepe and his men went into action. The wireless operator made a break for it, but was caught hiding under a bathtub in the basement of a nearby tenement. He turned out to be Johann Wenzel, a German Communist who had been on the Gestapo's black list for years. He was tortured until he agreed to collaborate with the Germans. In September 1942, he began transmitting to Moscow again – this time under Gestapo control. The following January, however, he managed to escape from his tormentors. Wenzel made it across the Dutch border, and remained in hiding in the Netherlands until the end of the war.

The Red Orchestra's Belgian circuit had been blown. So too, shortly afterwards, was the Dutch part of its operations. As more and more of its agents were rounded up, Piepe made some unwelcome discoveries. One was that the office next door to his in Brussels had been the headquarters of the man the Red Orchestra called their *Petit Chef*, the elusive *Grand Chef's* deputy. Even more alarming was the discovery of two messages to the GRU that Wenzel had not had time to encipher before he was arrested.

One of the messages listed German tank and aircraft production statistics in detail and recorded losses suffered on the Eastern Front. The other was more damaging still. It detailed the German order of battle for Case Blue, the German summer offensive intended to capture Stalingrad and the Russian oil fields in the Caucasus, giving in addition full details of its strategic planning and operational intentions. Both of them demonstrated just how deeply the Red Orchestra had penetrated into the higher echelons of the Third Reich.

It was obvious that somebody closely connected with the Wehrmacht High Command was supplying the Red Orchestra with top-secret information. The question was who? The news that there was a nest of spies at work hit the Germans like the proverbial thunderbolt. Hitler himself ordered the Abwehr, the Gestapo and SS counterintelligence to redouble their efforts to track down the traitors whatever the cost. The one reassuring fact – or so the Germans thought – was that Wenzel had not had the time to transmit the Case Blue message to Moscow before his capture. In fact, though they were totally unaware of it, the Red Orchestra's Swiss network had already transmitted the text of Hitler's Directive No. 14, which set out all Case Blue's strategic objectives, independently to Moscow.

Above: A patriot to the core, Grand Admiral Alfred von Tirpitz was German's Navy Minister during the First World War. His great-nephew, Harro Schulze-Boysen, codenamed Choro, was the driving force behind the Red Orchestra's Berlin circuit.

It was now that the Germans had an unexpected stroke of luck. The Abwehr cryptologists finally succeeded in breaking the Red Orchestra's ciphers. On 14 July 1942, they successfully decoded a message Moscow had transmitted to the Petit Chef in Brussels in October the previous year. It provided the Germans with the breakthrough they had been seeking so desperately. Moscow had committed a fatal blunder.

Worried by an apparent breakdown in radio communications, the GRU had transmitted the home addresses of three of the leading members of the Red Orchestra's Berlin circuit over the air, ordering the Petit Chef to go to Berlin and contact them. Within two days, the Gestapo had identified them. They were Lieutenant Harro Schulze-Boysen, a Luftwaffe communications officer in the Air Ministry, Dr Alfred Harnack, a senior civil servant in the Ministry of Economics and Dr Adam Kuckholt, a well-known writer.

Both Schulze-Boysen and Harnack were well-connected – the former was the grand-nephew of Grand Admiral Alfred von Tirpitz, who had built the Imperial High Seas Fleet for Kaiser Wilhelm II, while the latter was the scion of a famous academic family. All three men had been recruited by Alexander

Korotov, a GRU agent who had been working as Third Secretary in the Soviet Embassy in Berlin, as far back as 1939.

Despite the best efforts of Horst Heilmann, a Red Orchestra operative planted in the Funkabwehr cryptology section, to warn him he had been unmasked, the unsuspecting Schulze-Boysen was arrested in the Air Ministry on 30 August. Libertas, his wife, who had promptly gone into hiding, was caught a few days later trying to board a train at the Anhalter railway station. Harnack and Mildred Harnack-Fish, his American-born wife, were seized by the Gestapo on 7 September while they were breakfasting at the hotel where they were taking their summer vacation. In total, 117 operatives, informants and couriers followed them into Gestapo custody.

Schulze-Boysen, Harnack and their wives, plus Heilmann, the group's two radio operator and seven others, were put on trial on 16 December 1942. All but four of them were condemned to death. Mildred Harnack was one of the latter, having been sentenced to six years imprisonment, but she did not escape Hitler's vengeance for long. By his personal order, she was retried, sentenced to death and guillotined on 16 February 1943. Her husband and the two Schulze-Boysens had perished already. They were executed on 22 December.

While the Gestapo in Berlin was rounding up the Red Orchestra spies in the capital, Piepe and his SS colleague Karl Giering had shifted their operations from Brussels to Paris. Their priority target was the elusive Grand Chef, but he proved impossible to track down. The Petit Chef appeared to be more accessible. They were tipped off that he had fled south to Marseilles, taking his mistress with him.

Unfortunately for Piepe and Giering, Marseilles was in the Vichy-administered Unoccupied Zone and they had no jurisdiction there. In November 1942, however, German troops moved into the whole of the southern part of the country. The Gestapo quickly followed. On 12 November, a snatch squad raided the luxury apartment in which the Petit Chef and his lover were living, arrested both of them and escorted them back to Paris. They were then transferred to Brussels and finally to Berlin where, after four days of interrogation at Gestapo headquarters, the Petit Chef broke and turned traitor. As well as disclosing full details of the Red Orchestra's French operations, he was forced to reveal his true identity. He was Viktor Sukulov-Gurevich, a GRU captain, who had been working for the Grand Chef in Brussels since 1939.

Armed with this invaluable information, the hunt for the Grand Chef intensified. On 27 November Piepe and Giering arrested him in Paris while he was being treated by his dentist. He turned out to be Leopold Trepper, a Polish Jew, who had been working undercover for the GRU in Paris, arriving there for the first time in 1937. The next year, he had been chosen by General Ivan Terenchevich Peresypkin, the GRU's director, to become the head of Soviet espionage operations in Western Europe.

Trepper was quick to come to terms with his captors. Though later he claimed that his willingness to cooperate with them was a ruse to give him time to work out a plan of escape, the information he supplied enabled the Germans to wipe out the Red Orchestra's whole French circuit. Nor did he share his luckless subordinates' fate. Those who were not executed were shipped to Germany where, together with the operatives from the Belgian circuit, they were shipped to Mauthausen Concentration Camp near Linz in Austria. Only a handful survived.

Above: Boysen poses in his Luftwaffe uniform. His job at the Air Ministry – Goering himself gave him the post – meant that he had access to all kinds of highly-classified military information.

The Grand Chef, by contrast, was set up in an imposing mansion in the Parisian suburb of Neuilly. There, joined by the Petit Chef and a few other turncoats, he played what the Germans had christened a *Funkspiel* (radio game) with Moscow. The aim was to fool the GRU into giving away details of other Comintern spies and French Communist party activists working against the Germans in France. In September 1943, however, Trepper managed to escape his captors and go on the run. He remained in hiding until after the Allied liberation of Paris in August 1944.

It was not the end of the story. Just as the Red Orchestra's Berlin circuit was being broken up and the Grand Chef was becoming a turncoat after his detention in France, the Germans started to detect more coded radio messages – this time originating from Switzerland. Three transmitters were in daily contact with Moscow, two being located in Geneva and the other in Lausanne.

The Swiss apparat, as the GRU called it, was headed by Sandor Rado, a Hungarian who had been operating in Switzerland since 1936. There was little the Germans could do directly to put a stop to its activities; eventually, it was the Swiss themselves, who, fearful that Hitler might order his troops to invade their country, acted to silence the transmitters. The Swiss police struck in Geneva first. Then they moved in on the transmitter in Lausanne.

It did not end there. In May 1944, the Swiss arrested Rudolf Rossler, a German refugee publisher. Based in Lucerne and therefore codenamed 'Lucy', he was Rador's most important agent. His high-level contacts within the Wehrmacht – most importantly Lieutenant-General Fritz Thiele in the communications department of the War Ministry – had passed him a wealth of invaluable information, including the full plan for Operation Citadel, Hitler's last attempt to regain the strategic initiative on the Eastern Front. Rossler's usefulness was now at an end.

After he was released on bail that September, Rossler lacked the means to re-establish contact with Moscow. He had also lost most of his informants, many of whom had been executed for taking part in the abortive July Bomb Plot to assassinate the Fuehrer.

Right: A German panzer crew pause for a rest during the 1943 battle of Kursk. They might have looked less relaxed had they known that the Red Orchestra had supplied Moscow with the complete plans for the operation.

Opposite: The liberation of Paris in 1944 meant that Trepper, who had been in hiding since escaping from the Germans, could finally walk free. But back in Russia he was accused of being a double agent.

THE MISSION TO KILL A MONSTER

Operation Anthropoid

Two brave patriots gave their own lives to kill Reinhard Heydrich, the Nazi commander of Czechoslovakia – but at a terrible cost

IN THE CRYPT of the Saints Cyril and Methodius Cathedral in central Prague, on 18 June 1942, the last of the Czech parachutists were cornered, but still fighting, after a six-hour battle. SS troopers used tear gas to try to flush them out and even called out the Prague Fire Brigade to pump water into the crypt and flood it. But the Czechs who survived the onslaught refused to surrender, choosing suicide over the inevitability of humiliation and a cruel death. They died content that Operation Anthropoid had been successful and that an unspeakably cruel monster was dead.

Having already taken control of the Sudetenland, a predominantly German-speaking part of Czechoslovakia, at the end of September 1938 – with the acquiescence of Britain, France and Italy through the Munich Agreement – Hitler grew ever more confident. Through a mixture of devious

FACT FILE

BORN: Main participants – Free Czech parachutists Jan Kubiš, born 24 June 1913 in Dolní Vilémovice, Moravia (now Czech Republic); Josef Gabčik, born 8 April 1912 in Palosnya (now Poluvsie), Slovakia

DIED: Both on 18 June 1942

MISSION: To kill Reinhard Heydrich, the SS *Reichsprotector* of Bohemia and Moravia

INTELLIGENCE TECHNIQUES: Living undercover in occupied territory, liaising with resistance groups

FATE: After mortally wounding Heydrich on 27 May 1942, either died in the fighting or committed suicide to evade capture

LEGACY: Four films, four novels, non-fiction books, museums, memorials and the gratitude of a nation

diplomacy and the threat of overwhelming force, he was able to proclaim on 13 March 1939 that Czechoslovakia was now a German Protectorate. Later, he tried much the same trick with Poland, but this time triggered World War II. Nevertheless, he lost no time in putting the stamp of Nazism on Czechoslovakia.

Hitler entrusted the task to SS *Obergruppenführer* Reinhard Heydrich, a 37-year-old died-in-the-wool Nazi, whom Hitler described as 'the man with the iron heart'. Heydrich was one of the main architects of the Holocaust:

'We have racially inferior people but with good judgement, then we have racially unacceptable people with bad judgement. As to the first kind, we must resettle them in the Reich or somewhere else, but we have to make sure they no longer breed ... One group remains, though, these people are racially acceptable but hostile in their thinking ... We can relocate some of them into the Reich ... and then Germanize and re-educate them. If this cannot be done, we must put them against the wall.'

In reality, Heydrich did not bother too much about relocating people and re-educating them. He introduced his so-called 'whip and sugar' policy. This meant that those who co-operated were fed and that those who did not would die. In general, Jews, Romany gypsies, homosexuals and intellectuals were killed anyway.

Above: Reinhard Heydrich, Himmler's deputy and head of the Reich's Security Services, so impressed Hitler through his efficiency and ruthlessness that he hailed him as 'the best of the young National Socialists'.

For the Czech Government in Exile, based in London and headed by former President Edvard Beneš, it was too much to bear. Something must be done, they thought, to encourage resistance in their homeland, keep the resistance movement under their control, and put a halt – however temporary – to Heydrich's bloodletting: the answer, they decided, was to assassinate him.

With the co-operation of Britain's Special Operations Executive, a number of Czech soldiers were recruited; all had escaped from Czechoslovakia following the German assault. Warrant Officer Josef Gabčik and Staff Sergeant Karel Svoboda were to carry out the killing itself, supported by Adolf Opálka (the Commanding Officer), Jan Kubiš, Josef Bubli, Karel Čurda, Jan Hruby,

Right: A Handley Page Halifax bomber dropped the band of Czech parachutists charged with killing Heydrich into Czechoslovakia. SOE had planned the mission down to the last detail.

Jaroslav Svarc, Viliam Gerik and Josef Valčík; some of these were already or soon would be in Czechoslovakia. At first they were stationed with the 'Free Czechoslovaks' – other Czech soldiers who formed an army in exile – at Cholmondeley Castle, in Cheshire, England, before attending a parachute course in Manchester.

There Svoboda suffered a head injury during a jump, and his place was taken in the lead team, alongside Gabčik, by Jan Kubiš, who had already been awarded the Croix de Guerre while fighting with the French Army during the first campaign of the War. Their training was completed at the SOE Special Course in Scotland and at SOE's Section XVII in Brickendonbury Manor, Hertford, where they learnt to use explosives and were also taught sabotage techniques.

At 10pm on Sunday 28 December 1941, Kubiš, Gabčik and their comrades, laden with guns and explosives and carrying false papers, climbed into a Handley-Page Halifax Mk II bomber at RAF Tangmere, near Chichester, West Sussex. Each man had written his last will and testament, and had previously signed a pledge, recorded by The Holocaust Education and Archive Research Team (HEART): 'The substance of my mission is that I shall be sent back to my homeland ... in order to commit an act of sabotage or terrorism at a place and a situation depending on our findings ... I will do so effectively so as to generate the sought-after response not only in the home country but also abroad. I will do it to the extent of my best knowledge and conscience ... '

Things did not go well at first: snow led to the aircraft missing the drop zone and the team landed at the village of Nehvizdy, east of Prague. But they made their way via Pilsen to Prague, where they contacted members of the resistance movements and some paratroopers who had been involved in other missions.

First, they had to reconnoitre the ground and work out how, where and when Heydrich could be killed. They had a number of ideas, all of which seemed on examination to be impracticable: first, to blow Heydrich up on a train; and, second, to put a cable across a road often used by Heydrich – this idea was tried, but failed to work because Heydrich's car

FEROCIOUS REPRISALS

HITLER'S RESPONSE TO the news of Heydrich's assassination was immediate, decisive and characteristically savage. Telling the SS and Gestapo to 'wade in blood' to find the killers, he ordered that as many as 30,000 Czechs should be killed and that, in any villages found to have harboured or helped the assassins:

all men and boys over 15 should be killed;
all women should be sent to a concentration camp;
all children suitable for 'Aryanization' should be sent to Germany and raised by SS families
the village should be razed to the ground.

The SS set to with gusto. According to the Holocaust Education and Archive Research Team (HEART), they raided 5,000 villages and towns and arrested 3,180 people – of whom 1,344 were sentenced to be executed. Fortunately, Hitler's target of 30,000 victims was never reached.

For some reason the village of Lidice, around 12 miles west of Prague, was singled out for retribution, even though there was only the flimsiest of evidence against its inhabitants. Early in the morning of 10 June 1942, SS men rounded up 173 men and boys – all the male inhabitants – and shot them in groups of ten against a barn wall. The women and children fared little better: 184 women were sent to Ravensbrück Concentration Camp, where few, if any, survived; 88 children were taken to Poland, where a few were selected for Aryanization – the rest were sent to Chelmno (known to the Germans as 'Kulmhof') Extermination Camp, where they were gassed on arrival.

But the German retribution was not yet over. According to HEART: 'After them came engineers with charges to blow up the still-standing walls, then pioneers with bulldozers who flattened the ruins, uprooted the fruit trees and filled in the lake; they even diverted the stream.' Lidice's inhabitants did not go unburied, though – 30 Jews en route to a concentration camp were diverted to dig a common grave before they resumed their journey to their own deaths.

The atrocity at Lidice is still fairly well remembered, partly because the SS made a film of what they had done, and it can still be seen at a museum near the rebuilt village. But two weeks later, much the same thing happened at Ležáky, a hamlet consisting of eight houses and a mill, where the SS had found a British radio set. Ležáky was never rebuilt.

Left: This painting –
though not a wholly
accurate depiction
– captures the moment
when Heydrich's
Mercedes staff car
was attacked on the
outskirts of Prague.

Above: The Orthodox Cathedral of Saints Cyril and Methodius where seven of the Czech parachutists who had assassinated Heydrich died on 18 June 1942 after a 14-hour shoot-out with the SS and the Gestapo.

never appeared. Finally, however, Heydrich himself gave them the ideal opportunity. He moved out of his lodging in Prague Castle to occupy a nearby chateau, but each morning he had to drive from the chateau to his headquarters. And his route took him via a steep right-handed turn in the Prague suburbs at which his driver had to slow down – even better, there was a tram stop just by it at which the assassins could wait without arousing suspicion. The die was cast.

On the morning of 27 May, Heydrich's driver, SS *Oberscarführer* Johannes Kien, duly slowed down for the turn. Josef Gabčik and Jan Kubiš were in position, with Valěík and Opálka acting as lookouts. Gabčik stepped in front of the car and tried to open up a Sten submachine gun that had been hidden beneath his overcoat – it jammed. But before the Germans could reach their weapons, Kubiš threw an anti-tank grenade at the car. It exploded, filling the car with shrapnel, and the wounds it caused were contaminated by horse hair from the filling of its upholstery. Klein jumped out of the car to chase Kubiš, who had splinter injuries from the bomb, but was ordered by the injured Heydrich, who was firing his own pistol, to chase Gabčik – Klein did so, only for Gabčik to shoot him twice. The Anthropoid team fled to safe houses, believing their attempt had failed.

Meanwhile, Heydrich was taken to the Na Bulovce Hospital where his injuries were treated. It was thought that he would make a full recovery but his condition deteriorated gradually until he fell into a coma and died on 4 June. The post mortem states that sepsis was

responsible, but several commentators have suggested that he was killed by botulism, with which the anti-tank grenade had been deliberately infected. It is not impossible as the grenade was described as being 'specially modified' and was seen to be covered with tape; the British were thought to have been experimenting with botulinum poison. The SOE files remain sealed so the truth is not yet known.

Above: Heydrich's wrecked staff car. The grenade the second assassin threw exploded against the right rear wing, blasting a large hole in the bodywork.

Even before Heydrich's death, Hitler's fury had made the arrest of the fighters a top priority for every SS and Gestapo man. After it, the pressure from Berlin intensified. Success was not long in coming: Karel Čurda was arrested by the Gestapo and persuaded – with a bribe of 1 million Reichsmarks – to give them a list of all the team's contacts in Prague. On 17 June, the Gestapo raided the flat of the Moravec family: Mrs Moravec bit into a cyanide capsule, but her 17-year-old son, Ata, still refused to talk – until that is, they filled him with brandy and showed him his mother's severed head in a fish tank. Ata told them everything they wanted to know.

The next day, 700 SS troops surrounded the Sts Cyril and Methodius Cathedral where the paratroopers were hiding. After a fierce two-hour gun battle, Opálka, Svarc and Kubiš lay dead in the body of the Cathedral – the latter had been wounded and then shot himself. Valčík, Hruby, Gabčik and Bublik were holed up in the crypt in an almost impregnable position, so long as they had sufficient ammunition. They survived gunfire, tear gas and flooding, and killed 14 SS troopers; they even tried to dig their way out through a tunnel. Eventually, they could do no more. Rather than surrender, they shot themselves.

Operation Anthropoid was no more – but neither was Reinhard Heydrich. The brave Czech soldiers had died for their cause but thought it was a price worth paying.

Operation Mincemeat

In spring 1943, two British intelligence officers came up with a cunning scheme. Its aim was to fool Hitler into believing that the planned invasion of Sicily would fall elsewhere. Operation Mincemeat was the result

FACT FILE

CONCEIVED: April/May, 1943

MISSION: Planting false documents on the body of a dead British officer and getting them into enemy hands so that the Axis High Command would believe that the Allies intended to strike in Sardinia and Greece, rather than Sicily, which was their real target

INTELLIGENCE TECHNIQUES: False identity, fake and forged documentation

FATE: Accomplished as planned. The dead 'Major' was buried with full military honours in Spain, where the body had been washed ashore

LEGACY: Generally considered to have been one of the most successful deceptions in the history of warfare

WITH THE AXIS position in North Africa crumbling – the final capitulation in Tunisia took place on 13 May 1943 – the question was where and when would the Allies strike next? There was no doubt that Hitler and Mussolini had suffered a shattering defeat. Between them, they had lost 950,000 troops – killed, wounded or captured – plus 2,400,000 gross tons of shipping, 6,200 guns, 2,550 tanks and 70,000 trucks during the course of the North African campaign.

Sicily, and then the Italian mainland, were the prime Allied targets. The problem

was, as Winston Churchill famously put it, 'everyone but a bloody fool would know it was Sicily'. Hitler was far from being that. What the Allies had to do was to convince the Fuehrer that the coming blow would fall elsewhere, so that he would divert reinforcements away from the island ready to drive the Allies back into the sea if they attempted to land in some other strategic hotspot.

The notion of planting supposedly top-secret military documents on a dead man's body and letting them fall into German hands was conceived by two British officers – Lieutenant-Commander Ewen Montagu, a former lawyer who was now a backroom wizard of British naval intelligence, and Flight-Lieutenant Charles Cholmondeley, a bespectacled 25-year-old RAF officer attached to MI5. Which of the two actually had the initial idea is uncertain, but they both worked together in perfecting the plan. The scheme, as it developed, turned into a classic example of double bluff.

Above: Ewen Montagu, a clever, well-connected lawyer before the war, was the driving force behind Operation Mincemeat, which he turned from a paper speculation into a practical reality.

Montagu and Cholmondeley did not intend simply to divert enemy attention away from the actual invasion target. They were more ambitious than that. They aimed to convince the Germans that any attack on Sicily would be a decoy – a prelude to another major invasion effort that would be launched elsewhere. The question was whether the intricate plot they were devising would successfully throw the enemy off-guard.

Both men decided right from the start that just any old body would not serve their purposes. Their corpse, they believed, must have a name, a personality and a past in order to be passed off as a credible military courier. Captain (Acting Major) William Martin, was their Frankenstein-like creation from start to finish. Everything from his likes and dislikes, his habits and hobbies, his strengths and his weaknesses, right down to the underclothes he wore beneath his uniform were the result of careful discussion and debate between the two of them. They were determined that Martin would be perfect down to the smallest detail.

The documentation Martin carried in a locked briefcase attached by a clip to the belt of the trenchcoat he would be wearing was equally convincing. The key items were two highly-secret letters – one from General Sir Archibald Nye, vice-chief of the Imperial General Staff to General Sir Harold Alexander, the British commander-in-chief in Tunisia, and the other from Vice-Admiral Lord Louis Mountbatten, head of Combined Operations in London, to Admiral Sir Andrew Cunningham, commander-in-chief of Britain's Mediterranean Fleet. Both letters were masterpieces of deception. They confirmed that the Allied forces massing in North Africa were preparing to attack Sardinia and the Greek Peloponnese. Any landings in Sicily, they revealed, would simply be in the nature of a diversion.

Cholmondeley and Montagu called the plan Operation Trojan Horse. It was rechristened Operation Mincemeat at a later date, by which time

Montagu was deeply involved in its detailed planning. At the end of March, 1943, he was finally given the official go-ahead to proceed with the plan.

Keeping the corpse well-preserved enough to pass muster presented its problems. Montagu managed to find a refrigeration unit in which it could be kept safe in cold storage. Taking a photograph of it for Martin's Marine identity card was also problematic. 'I defy anyone to take a photograph of someone who is dead and make it look as if he could conceivably be alive', Montagu wrote after the war. Chance provided the solution: at a meeting, Montagu met a man 'who might have been the twin brother of the corpse'. Getting a photograph of Martin's supposed fiancée proved easier. Jean Leigh, a clerk in MI5, obligingly provided a snapshot of herself posing on a beach.

Above: Charles Cholmondeley never got the full credit he deserved for originally suggesting the plan for Operation Mincemeat. Like Montagu, he possessed what Churchill called a 'corkscrew mind'.

On 28 April 1943, Martin was put on board the submarine *Seraph*, packed in a special steel container filled with dry ice. *Seraph* immediately set sail, on a two-day voyage, making for Huerta, a city on the Atlantic coast of southern Spain. Riddled with Axis sympathizers, the country was the natural choice of destination.

The decision, indeed, may have been triggered by an accident the previous September. Shortly before Operation Torch, the Allied invasion of French North Africa, was launched, an RAF Catalina flying boat crashed off Cadiz. The body of a passenger killed in the accident and carrying a letter containing the date for the projected landings was recovered by the Spanish authorities. They passed the information over to the Germans, who for whatever reason chose to ignore it. Montagu and Cholmondeley were confident that the enemy, having missed that earlier golden opportunity, would this time be far more likely to act on the information they were planting. Martin, they hoped, would be taken for a military courier who had drowned after the aircraft flying him to Gibraltar had come down in the sea.

Above: The Royal Navy submarine *Seraph* gets under way. At the start of her voyage to the Spanish coast, only Lieutenant Norman Jewell, her commander, knew exactly what her special cargo was.

On 30 April at 4:30am, *Seraph* cautiously surfaced about a mile off the Spanish coast. A working party hauled the heavy canister on deck – its members had been told that it contained top secret meteorological equipment. Then everyone apart from the submarine's officers was ordered below. As dawn began to break, Lieutenant Norman L.A. (Bill) Jewell, the submarine's commander, told them what their mission really was and swore them to secrecy. Martin's body was then transferred from the canister onto the deck, where he was fitted with his life jacket and chained to his briefcase. Jewell read the 39th Psalm aloud as the corpse was slipped gently into the sea, where, driven by the tide, it slowly started to drift towards the shore. *Seraph* quickly submerged and set off for its home port.

At around 9.30am, a fisherman out trawling for sardines came across the waterlogged corpse drifting in the sea. He hauled the body onto his boat, headed for the beach and brought it ashore.

The Spanish authorities in Huelva reported the news of the discovery to the British Embassy in Madrid, but not before Adolf Clauss, the local agent of the Abwehr, had been informed. He quickly passed on the information

THE MAN WHO NEVER WAS

CREATING A FALSE identity for 'the man who never was' and compiling the bogus documentation he carried involved weeks of painstaking work as British Intelligence slowly amassed an imposing collection of personal effects to help to bring 'Major William Martin' of the Royal Marines to life. As well as a military identity card, the faked documents included personal letters – one from Martin's father, two from 'Pam', his supposed fiancée, and a fourth from the family solicitor – a snapshot of his fiancée (pictured), a bill from a leading West End jeweller for an engagement ring and another one for accommodation from the Naval & Military Club, two theatre ticket stubs and a used bus ticket. A stern letter from Martin's bank manager asked him for the immediate repayment of his overdraft.

Finding a suitable corpse was obviously a top priority. Montagu started the search by consulting Sir Bernard Spilsbury, Britain's most celebrated forensic pathologist. Spilsbury reassured him that, because people died in air crashes for a variety of reasons, it was not essential to find a corpse that had perished by drowning. Montagu then turned to William Bentley Purchase, the coroner for the St Pancras district of London, to help him in his macabre quest. Albeit somewhat reluctantly, Purchase produced a suitable body – or so Montagu said.

For the rest of his life – he died in 1985 – Montagu kept the corpse's real identity a secret. In 2003, however, former police officer Colin Gibbon claimed that William Martin was in fact Tom Martin, a sailor on the escort carrier *Dasher* who perished in a massive internal explosion on the ship just off the coast of Scotland in March 1943. Montagu, so it was alleged, abstracted the body of the other Martin before it could be buried in a mass grave with the other victims of the explosion. The following year, John Melville, one of Tom Martin's fellow sailors, was publically named by a Royal Navy officer as 'the man who never was'.

In 2011, Professor Denis Smyth, a Toronto University historian, came up with fresh evidence. The corpse, said Smith, was definitely that of Glyndwr Michael, a 34-year-old alcoholic Welsh vagrant who committed suicide in London in January 1943. His corpse had been handed over to Montagu by Purchase. Smyth had unearthed a hitherto overlooked memorandum written by Montagu in which he stated that the rat poison Michael had swallowed could not be detected by a post-mortem and that therefore neither the Spanish – nor the Germans – would ever establish the true cause of death.

Proponents of the Dasher theory still remained unconvinced. They argued that the body of an alcoholic tramp could never have been passed off successfully as that of a smart Royal Marine officer. Only Montagu knew the truth – and he took its secret with him to his grave.

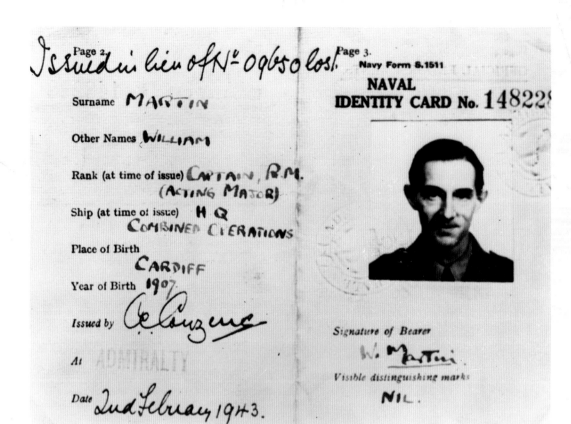

Page 2. *Issued in lieu of Nᵒ 09650 lost.* Page 3. Navy Form S.1511

Surname MARTIN

Other Names WILLIAM

Rank (at time of issue) CAPTAIN, R.M. (ACTING MAJOR)

Ship (at time of issue) HQ COMBINED OPERATIONS

Place of Birth CARDIFF

Year of Birth 1907

Issued by *[signature]*

At ADMIRALTY

Date 2nd February 1943.

NAVAL IDENTITY CARD No. 148229

Signature of Bearer W. Martin.

Visible distinguishing marks NIL.

Above: Acting Major William Martin's Royal Marine identity card. To add a further note of authenticity it is a replacement, suggesting Martin had been careless enough to lose the original.

to his own superiors. In the meantime, the Spanish organized a hasty post-mortem. It was concluded that Martin had indeed drowned. Two days later, he was buried in the city cemetery. His briefcase and personal effects were sent for safe-keeping to naval headquarters in the Spanish capital. The navy passed them on to the Spanish General Staff.

The plot then thickened. The British pressed for the immediate return of the briefcase. The Spanish eventually obliged, but, in the meantime, the Abwehr had got its hands on the briefcase's contents and hastily photographed them. It also examined the personal effects. Once the photographs had been taken, the documents the briefcase contained were carefully reinserted in their original envelopes, re-sealed and the briefcase returned to the Spanish to hand back to the British, apparently untouched.

The German Embassy in Madrid radioed the contents of the letters to Berlin and rushed the photographs to OKW headquarters, where they were examined by Admiral Wilhelm Canaris, the head of the Abwehr, Hitler's

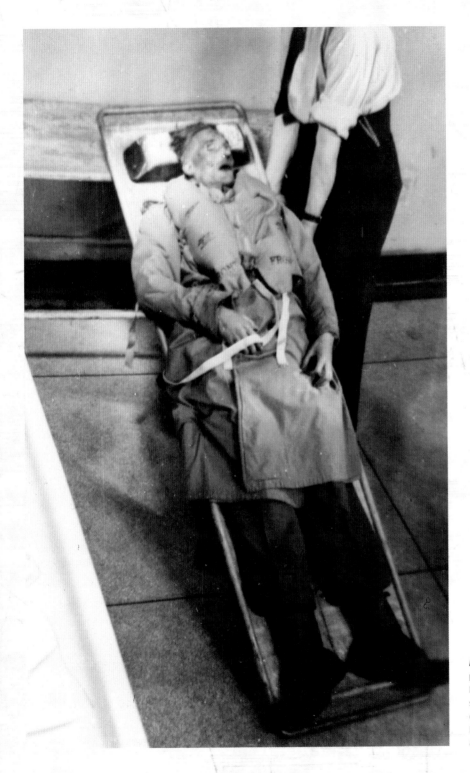

Left: A still from the post-war film 'The Man Who Never Was' shows Martin's body, dressed ready to be lowered into the sea, in a mortuary.

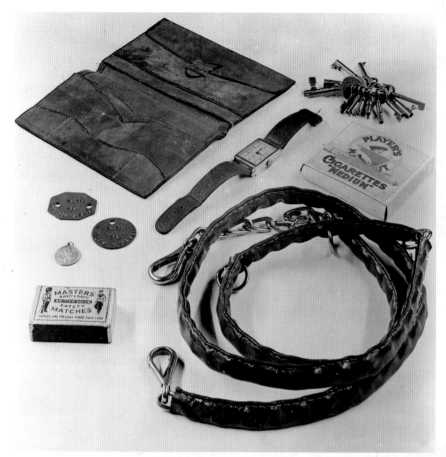

Right: : A selection of personal effects carried on Martin's body. As well as a somewhat battered wallet, they included a St Christopher's medallion and a special belt that secured his briefcase to his greatcoat.

top military commanders and by the Fuehrer himself. Initially, at least, he questioned whether Martin's corpse might be an Allied plant, but was soon convinced that he had been a genuine courier. It followed logically that the information in the letters in the briefcase must also be correct.

Hitler acted immediately. On 12 May, he reorganized German defensive priorities throughout the Mediterranean. 'Measures regarding Sardinia and the Peloponnese', he ordered, 'take precedence over everything else'. Three panzer divisions – one from France and two from the Eastern Front – were rushed to Greece and Rommel despatched to take over command of German forces in the region. Mussolini's protests that Sicily remained the obvious Allied target were dismissed out of hand. General Alfred Jodl, the Wehrmacht's head of operations, was overhead bellowing down the telephone to the German military attaché in Rome, 'You can forget about

Sicily. We know it is Greece.' More and more troops and military equipment were hastily shifted to be ready to meet and beat the Allied invading forces when they attempted to land.

The British, for their part, were carefully examining the briefcase and its contents to see if they had been tampered with. Despite all the precautions the Abwehr had taken, they soon discovered that this, indeed, had been the case. Instead of being thrown into a state of panic, the opposite was the case. Hitler had reacted just as British Intelligence had hoped. Churchill, who had been in on the plan, was immediately signalled: 'Mincemeat swallowed hook, line and sinker.' He, too, was overjoyed. Planning for the invasion of Sicily went full steam ahead. As for the supposed Major Martin, he had never existed. He was truly 'the man who never was'.

Left: Snerlock Holmes-style pipe in hand, Ewen Montagu poses for the press in New York in 1954. He had just arrived in the city to promote the US publication of "The Man Who Never Was," his own book about Operation Mincemeat.

Operation Valkyrie

The July 1944 bomb plot to assassinate Hitler at his Wolf's Lair headquarters near Rastenburg in East Prussia was the closest anyone ever got to killing him. It was the fourteenth time an assassin had tried to eliminate the Fuehrer

IT WAS A hot, sultry July day in East Prussia as preparations got underway for the customary military briefing held every morning at the Wolf's Lair, Adolf Hitler's field headquarters buried deep in the forest four miles or so away from Rastenburg. Today, in addition to the usual members of the Wehrmacht's high command, there was an extra officer in attendance. He was Colonel Count Klaus von Stauffenberg, the recently-appointed Chief of Staff to General Friedrich Fromm, commander-in-chief of the Reserve Army. He was a war hero, who had lost his left eye and hand plus two fingers from his right hand during the fighting in Tunisia the previous year.

Stauffenberg had arrived from Berlin ostensibly to outline what reinforcements the Reserve Army could provide to prop up the troops desperately resisting the

FACT FILE

DATE: 20 July 1944

MISSION: To assassinate the Fuehrer at Wolf's Lair, Rastenburg, East Prussia, then implement Operation Valkyrie to overthrow the Nazis, and bring Germany under military and ultimately civilian control

INTELLIGENCE TECHNIQUE: Assassination

FATE: The attempt failed and Hitler escaped with only superficial wounds. The principal plotters were shot by troops loyal to the regime after the attempted uprising in Berlin had been suppressed. They were sentenced to death by Colonel-General Friedrich Fromm, the commander-in-chief of the Reserve Army, in a desperate attempt to cover up his own prior knowledge of the plot

Above: Officers at Wolf's Lair talk anxiously amongst themselves. One of the crucial mistakes the July bomb-plotters made was not to sever communications between the Wolf's Lair and the outside world.

Previous page: Hitler and Goering confer after the bombing. At first, both thought it was the work of a lone assassin but soon discovered it marked the start of an attempted military coup.

Soviet advance on the crumbling central sectors of the Eastern Front. He, however, had a different agenda. A leading member of the military conspiracy to remove the Nazis from power, he had resolved to take this opportunity to assassinate the Fuehrer.

Stauffenberg, accompanied by Lieutenant Werner von Haeften, his adjutant, had flown into the airfield at Rastenburg from Berlin at 10:15am that morning. He was immediately driven to the Wolf's Lair, while Haeften accompanied Major-General Helmuth Stieff, another conspirator, to army headquarters nearby. Later, he rejoined Stauffenberg, who had been attending a pre-briefing meeting with Field Marshal Wilhelm Keitel, head of the OKW (*Oberkommando der Wehrmacht*), in preparation for the conference with the Fuehrer.

As soon as Keitel's meeting broke up, Stauffenberg asked for permission to go and freshen up. He was told to be as quick as he could, since the time of Hitler's briefing had been brought forward. Haeften, carrying a bulky briefcase, met him in the corridor. As soon as both men were alone together in the toilet, they hastily started to prime the two bombs they had brought with them in the briefcase. Before they could set the fuses of the second one, Stauffenberg was summoned to join the Fuehrer's meeting. He told Haeften to get rid of the unprimed bomb.

The briefing had already begun when Stauffenberg was ushered into the wooden barrack, where it was being held in preference to the usual underground bunker. Hitler, who was seated alongside a long map-table, quickly shook hands before turning to listen again to Major-General Adolf Heusinger, who was delivering the customary Eastern Front situation report. Stauffenberg sat down as near to the Fuehrer as he could get, placing his briefcase under the table propped up against one of its legs. Then he muttered an excuse to leave to make an urgent telephone call. The conference went on without him.

The bomb detonated moments after Stauffenberg left the room. Hitler was bending over the map-table when it exploded. The windows and doors of the hut were blown out and clouds of smoke billowed up from the wreckage. Splinters of glass, pieces of wood and showers of paper and other debris flew in all directions. Parts of the wrecked hut caught fire.

Stauffenberg, who had witnessed the explosion from a safe distance, was convinced that no one could possibly have survived its blast. He and Haeften made for their staff car, bluffed their way through the two SS security cordons surrounding the Wolf's Lair and headed back to the airfield. They took off for Berlin both certain that the assassination attempt had been successful and that Hitler was dead.

Back at the Wolf's Lair, it was pandemonium. Cries for help echoed through the air. Some of the bomb's victims had been hurled to the floor or propelled across the room by the force of the blast. Human shapes stumbled around, concussed, partially blinded and with shattered eardrums, trying to get clear of the smoke and debris. The seriously injured lay prostrate in the wreckage. Dr Heinrich Beyer, Hitler's stenographer who had taken the full force of the explosion, had both his legs blown off. He died later that afternoon. Colonel Heinz Brandt lost a leg and died the next day, as did General Gunther Korton, the Luftwaffe's Chief of Staff. Major-General Rudolf Schmundt, Hitler's Wehrmacht Chief of Staff, lost an eye and a leg and suffered serious facial burns, dying some weeks later.

Hitler, however, was very much alive. Providentially for him, someone had moved Stauffenberg's briefcase further down the table, so that he had

Above: Goering, Martin Bormann and other Nazi bigwigs examine the wrecked conference barracks. Had Stauffenberg had the time to prime the second bomb, Hitler would almost certainly have been killed.

managed to escape the full force of the blast. Had Stauffenberg managed to prime both bombs or had the conference been held in the usual concrete bunker, the Fuehrer would have almost certainly perished. As it was, he suffered only relatively minor injuries. He limped to safety, trying to beat out the flames burning his trousers. He bumped into Keitel, who embraced him crying out almost hysterically 'My Fuehrer, you're alive, you're alive!'

Slowly, Hitler made his way back to his personal bunker. His right arm was swollen and painful – so much so that he could barely lift it. He had swellings and abrasions on his other arm, burns and blisters on his hands and legs, cuts on his forehead and burst eardrums. Otherwise, he had escaped unscathed.

Meanwhile, the leaders of the conspiracy in Berlin – chief among them General Friedrich Olbricht, Fromm's deputy, and General Ludwig Beck, Chief of the General Staff until his enforced retirement in 1938 – gathered at Replacement Army headquarters in the Bendlerstrasse to await confirmation from Rastenburg as to whether Hitler was alive or dead. General Erich Fellgiebel, one of the conspirators who was in charge of communications at the Wolf's Lair, was responsible for making the signal. He was then to cut all telecommunications with the outside world for as long as possible – and at least for a crucial couple of hours. Fellgiebel failed in both tasks. When he realized that Hitler had survived the explosion, he panicked. By the time Stauffenberg got back to Berlin, the news that the Fuehrer was still alive was starting to spread.

Above: General Ludwig Beck had begun conspiring against Hitler as early as 1938, alarmed by the Fuehrer's aggressive intentions towards Czechoslovakia. Had Valkyrie succeeded, he would have become head of state.

Nor had the conspirators activated Operation Valkyrie immediately, as had been planned. They had intended to subvert the original Valkyrie emergency operation, which had been personally approved by Hitler and was designed to be implemented if there was an uprising among the millions of forced labourers toiling in the Reich and a consequent breakdown of law and order. Using the pretext that the SS were taking advantage of the Fuehrer's death to seize control of the government, their plan was to mobilize Reserve Army units in and around Berlin, secure the capital, disarm the SS and arrest all the leading Nazis before taking over power themselves.

Hours of invaluable time were wasted while the conspirators dithered. Fromm tried to clarify the situation by telephoning Rastenburg himself. He got through to Keitel, who assured him that Hitler had survived the explosion. Rather than agreeing to activate Valkyrie, he attempted to arrest the conspirators. Stauffenberg, who by now had arrived back at the Bendlerstrasse, had him arrested instead. He and Olbricht set to work, sending out teletypes and telephoning key commands ordering Valkyrie to be implemented immediately. Colonel-General Erich Hoepner took over from Fromm as commander of the Replacement Army, while Field Marshal Erwin von Witzleben arrived to take over as commander-in-chief.

Though late, the coup seemed at last to be going according to plan. Then teletypes started pouring out of OKW headquarters at Rastenburg countermanding the conspirators' orders. Doubts grew by the minute as the confusion mounted. Some army units went into action, but others stopped dead in their tracks. In the Bendlerstrasse itself, things were becoming increasingly chaotic as the tide began to turn inexorably against the plotters.

In Berlin, Major Otto Remer, the 32-year-old commander of the crack Grossdeutschland Guard Battalion, emerged as the key figure in the crushing of the attempted putsch. Though an ardent Nazi, he obeyed the orders he had received from Major-General Paul von Hasse, the city commandant, to seal off the government quarter of the city. His next move, Hasse ordered, would be to take all the senior party figures he could find into protective custody. Goebbels, the Propaganda Minister, was top of Remer's list.

Below: The courtyard outside the former Bendler Block is where Olbricht, Stauffenberg and other leading conspirators were shot after the failure of the Valkyrie coup.

The Minister was enjoying his customary afternoon siesta when he was awoken by an urgent telephone call from the Wolf's Lair alerting him to the failed assassination attempt and the fact that a full-scale military coup was apparently in progress. As he looked out of the window, he could see that Remer's troops were already starting to surround the house. He asked to speak to the young guard commander.

Remer explained that, as Hitler was dead, he had no alternative but to obey the orders he had been given by his military superiors. Goebbels assured him that the information was false and the Fuehrer was alive. Using his direct line to the Wolf's Lair, which the conspirators had failed to have cut, just as they had failed to take control of Berlin's radio station, he asked for Hitler to be brought to the phone to speak to Remer personally.

Remer took the receiver. Immediately he stiffened to attention as he recognized the unmistakeable sound of Hitler's voice. The Fuehrer wasted no time on pleasantries. Promoting Remer on the spot to the rank of Colonel, he ordered him to restore order in the capital, arrest the plotters

Above: Major Otto Remer, commander of the key Guard's Battalion stationed in Berlin, who turned his troops on the conspirators after speaking to Hitler.

THE AFTERMATH

ONCE HITLER REALIZED the scale of the conspiracy against him, he was quick to order Himmler and the Gestapo to begin systematically liquidating his enemies. Over the following months, more than 7,000 alleged conspirators were rounded up. Out of these, up to 5,000 ended up dead – either executed or as suicides. Field Marshal Erwin Rommel was the most prominent among the latter. He chose to take poison rather than stand trial and face public disgrace. Officially, it was announced that he had died from the wounds he had received when his car was strafed by an Allied fighter-bomber in Normandy. Hitler gave him a state funeral.

The trials themselves began on 7 August. The first conspirators to be arraigned before the so-called People's Court were former Field Marshal Erwin von Witzleben, Colonel-General Erich Hoepner, Major-General Helmuth Stieff and four others. All seven were sentenced to death by hanging. Others followed them into the dock. Among them was Colonel-General Carl Heinrich von Stulpnagel, the one-time military governor of Occupied France. Having blinded himself in a suicide attempt, he was hauled into court on 20 August. Roland Friesler, the presiding judge, showed him no mercy. He was condemned to death and hanged the same day.

Hitler's lust for vengeance was still not satisfied. He had the executions filmed so that he could watch them at his leisure. They continued until almost the last days of the war.

and crush the conspiracy. Remer obeyed. His troops lifted their blockade and, by 9:00pm, were on their way to the Bendlerstrasse to root out the conspirators in their headquarters. Meanwhile, loyal Panzer units were also closing in on the city centre.

The putsch was falling apart even before Remer and his men arrived on the scene. In Paris, where Colonel-General Carl Heinrich von Stulpnagel had ordered the detention of all the SS, SD and Gestapo personnel in the French capital, Field Marshal Hans von Kluge, the commander-in-chief in France, had rescinded the order.

In the Bendlerstrasse, staff officers loyal to Fromm released him from his quarters where he was being held under guard. As Remer's troops broke into the Reserve Army building, a brief gun-fight erupted in its corridors during which Stauffenberg took a bullet in the shoulder. Fromm had the now-despondent putchists brought before him. After a drumhead court-martial lasting just a few minutes, he announced that Olbricht, Colonel Mertz von Quirnheim, Haeften and 'this Colonel whose name I will no longer mention' had been sentenced to immediate execution. Beck, who had already shot himself with a borrowed revolver, lay dying at Fromm's feet. He told one of his officers to finish him off. Hoepner, who had asked for a confidential word with Fromm, was led out into captivity.

The four conspirators were hustled downstairs into the courtyard in front of the building where a ten-man firing squad was waiting for them. Olbricht was executed first. Then it was Stauffenberg's turn. As the execution squad fired its first volley, Haeften flung himself into the line of fire and took the bullets aimed at his Colonel. He died instantly. The firing-squad readied itself again. This time, Stauffenberg was hit. As the shots rang out, he shouted 'Long Live our Sacred Germany!' Mertz von Quirnheim, the last to be executed, said nothing.

Shortly after midnight, Hitler broadcast to the nation. He told his people he was speaking to them for two reasons – first, to let them hear his voice and to reassure them that he was safe and well and second to tell them about a crime 'committed by a tiny clique of ambitious, unconscionable and criminally stupid officers' that was 'without parallel in German history'. He promised grimly that this 'tiny gang of criminal elements' would be 'mercilessly eradicated'. The coming weeks and months were to show that he was as good as his word.

Opposite: A tourist inspects what remains of the Wolf's Lair. Much of it was demolished by the Germans in 1945, when the Soviet Army's decisive breakthrough in the east forced Hitler to abandon the complex.

30 AU, T-Force and Operation Paperclip

They helped defeat Hitler and Japan, then gave the West a head start in the Cold War against the Eastern bloc

HITLER'S GERMANY WAS much better prepared for World War II than any of the countries that he would make his enemies. Unlike them, he knew exactly what he intended to happen and had spent many years building up both his military forces and the technological and industrial resources to support them. As a result, his forces were stronger, their tactics – based on the *blitzkrieg* philosophy of surprise, speed, mobility and encirclement – were superior and their technology was more advanced, especially when it came to encryption, submarines, torpedoes, mines and even rocket-development.

In March 1942, in a smoke-filled Room 39 of The Old Admiralty Building, overlooking Horse Guards Parade, in London, the Naval Intelligence staff knew that something

FACT FILE

CREATED: 30 Assault Unit following a 20 March 1942 memo by Ian Fleming; T-Force in May/June 1944, by order of Supreme Headquarters Allied Expeditionary Force (SHAEF)

MISSION: To carry out individual raids and also accompany regular troops in order to seize German technology and military and industrial intelligence; later, also to capture German scientists

INTELLIGENCE TECHNIQUES: Qualities, such as speed, pinpoint targeting and precision execution

FATE: Triumph. Secured military and industrial advantages in World War II; success in the 'Manhattan Project' (to build an atomic bomb) and gave the West major advantages in the Space Race

LEGACY: Much information is still classified

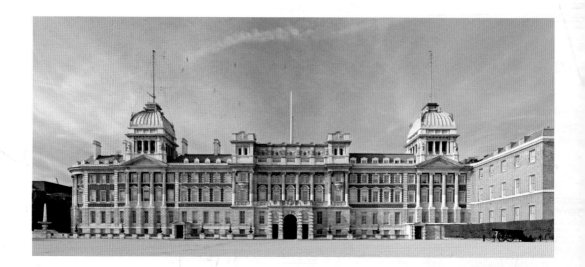

Above: The Old Admiralty Building, London, where Ian Fleming came up with the notion of setting up a special assault force, tasked with capturing top-secret enemy equipment and intelligence documentation.

Previous page: Walter Dornberger, Wernher von Braun, with his arm in plaster, and other leading scientists surrender to US troops in Austria in 1945.

must be done to catch up. It fell to Lieutenant Commander Ian Fleming, later to enjoy fame as the creator of James Bond, to come up with an idea to get Britain's technology back on terms: steal it. Under his direction, a special unit was set up, eventually to be called 30 Assault Unit (30AU), that would accompany raids against German positions and was specifically tasked with making off with any state-of-the-art equipment they could find as well as plans, designs and intelligence documents.

The first outing for 30AU was not a success: its troops were caught on the shore at the ill-fated Dieppe Raid in late 1942 and had to swim back to their boats. However, the Unit's work with Operation Torch, the invasion of North Africa in November 1942, was more productive: they captured the battle orders for the Italian and German fleets as well as code books and intelligence documents. After successful spells in Norway, the Greek Islands, Sicily, Corsica and Italy, 30AU returned to its base at Littlehampton, West Sussex, England, in November 1943 to prepare for the 'Second Front': the Allied assault on France. (In recognition of its service, 30AU's modern-day successors – 30 Commando Information Exploitation Group – were granted the 'freedom' of Littlehampton in 2013.)

The invasion of France, in June 1944, saw 30AU landing on Juno and Utah beaches 20 minutes after the first assault troops – under the names 'Woolforce' and 'Pikeforce' respectively (Pikeforce's leader was Captain RG Pike RM) – to attack the important German radar station at Douvres-la-Délivrande, before joining the assault on the French port of Cherbourg, stealing whatever it could, wherever it went. Next, it undertook operations around Rennes and Brest, before accompanying the Free French forces that liberated Paris; there its men blew open 80 safes to gather intelligence documents and captured the headquarters of Admiral Dönitz (Pike is said to have been the first Allied officer to drink at the bar of the Ritz Hotel). Then, carried in fast jeeps, 30AU marauded along the north coast of France, stripping intelligence and hardware from each port as it was captured.

By now, 30AU's success had impressed Allied High Command, and it was decided to broaden their activities – besides, as the Allies neared Germany and started to operate inside it, the pickings were likely to become even richer. As a result, T-Force was established in three groups: one was to accompany the Sixth United Army Group, operating in the south of France; another was to be with General Omar Bradley's 12th US Army Group, in the middle to north of France; and the third was to operate alongside the British 21st Army Group, in the north of France, Belgium and Holland.

Each T-Force was made up of a mixture of special forces and regular infantry. For example, T-Force for the 21st Army Group comprised, among others, 30AU along with the 5th Battalion The King's Liverpool Regiment and the 1st Battalion The Buckinghamshire Regiment. Apparently, it took a little time before the disparate units meshed together, as at first the strictly regimental soldiers' working practices were at odds with the somewhat devil-may-care attitudes of the special forces. Nevertheless, they managed to establish a mutual understanding, and the northern

Below: Operation Paperclip successfully brought many of Germany's top scientists to work in the USA. The group of rocket scientists here were photographed at Fort Bliss, Texas, where US rocket developments were centred.

Right: Like many other Paperclip scientists, any controversial episodes in von Braun's past were airbrushed out of existence before he was given a clean bill of political health to live and work in the USA.

T-force continued to fight – and steal – its way into Germany.

On 26 April 1945, T-Force took the German port of Bremen, after some hard fighting. There they seized U-boat pens along with 13 assembly lines on which new, more technologically advanced U-boats were to be built. They blew open 95 safes to capture intelligence papers – taking some 4 million Reichsmarks in the process – and also took the plant that made engines for the German's Focke-Wulf fighter planes. All this was vital, because at the time nobody knew how much technical advice the German had sent to Japan, with whom the Allies were still at war – neither did they know about the Allies' atomic bomb, which was to make such information redundant. Significantly, however T-Force also captured 13 German scientists, before moving on to Hamburg, where they did much the same thing.

Meanwhile, on 1 May, another part of T-Force, consisting of 30AU and the 5th King's, was making its way to the German naval base at Kiel – and it was vital that they took it as soon as possible because there was likely to be a stand-off with the advancing Russian forces. Although it had been agreed that Kiel would be under the control of the Western Allies, such were the technological riches to be plundered there that it was thought that the Russians might renege on their agreement. Besides, an armistice could only be a few days away.

So on 4 May, Major Tony Hibbert, in charge of 500 men of T-Force and

50 scientists who were there to assess any discoveries, advanced on Kiel as part of Operation Eclipse. Amid chaotic scenes, he took the naval base and, just as important, the Walterwerke Factory, a research and manufacturing installation in which the V1 and V2 rocket engines had been built.

The author Nicholas Rankin describes what T-Force found – a veritable soldiers' toyshop – in his book *Ian Fleming's Commandos: The Story of the Legendary 30 Assault Unit*, published by Oxford University Press:

' ... jet-driven explosive hydrofoils, radio-controlled glider bombs, remote controlled tankettes *[sic]*, rocket-propelled "sticky bombs", silent steam cannons, mine detonators and a new kind of big gun with a fuel injection system in the barrel to extend its range'.

'In a safe, they found a 16mm film of the new secret weapons that

SHAKEN, NOT STIRRED

JAMES BOND'S CREATOR, Ian Fleming, was a Commander in British Naval Intelligence during World War II, acting as Personal Assistant to Rear Admiral John Godfrey, its Director. (Later Fleming was to use Godfrey as the inspiration for 'M' in the James Bond books.) In September 1942, Fleming came up with the idea of setting up a commando force that would accompany raiding parties and have the specific function of stealing the enemy's technological secrets and intelligence documents – something that the German Naval Intelligence Division was already doing. Godfrey agreed, and the Special Intelligence Unit was born. 'Fleming's Red Indians', as its members were known in those politically incorrect days, had considerable success in operations in North Africa, the Mediterranean and Norway, and they were later renamed '30 Assault Unit' or '30AU'.

As the war progressed, the Allies set up T-Force to accompany their armies' advance through Europe, and 30AU played a prominent part in it. Fleming sat on the committee that selected its targets, which were recorded in 'Black Books' issued to the commander of each unit. 30AU was disbanded in 1946 and until fairly recently little was known about its activities with T-Force – much is still a mystery to this day.

But Fleming provided some clues in his James Bond novels, and in *Moonraker*, published in 1955, in particular. In 1945, T-Force, including 30AU, had taken the Walterwerke Factory in Kiel, north Germany, owned by a Dr Hellmuth Walter, where they captured a lethal collection of high-tech military equipment. In *Moonraker*, the main henchman of the villain, Sir Hugo Drax, is much like Dr Walter (who once worked for a German steel company called Rheinmetall-Borsig – a real company, it was also a target for T-Force). Walter has 50 German scientists working on Drax's rocket, said to be 'more or less all the guided-missile experts the Russians didn't get' – there is no mention of the ones that Britain and America got, perhaps because Fleming and T-Force had also 'co-opted' a fair number. And *Moonraker*, fuelled by hydrogen peroxide like Germany's V2 and said to look like it, was to be test-fired into the North Sea – just as V2s captured by T-Force had been fired into the North Sea in Operation Backfire, during October 1945.

So, as Fleming might have said about T-Force and 30AU: 'You only live twice.'

Germany was working on, which had been shown to Hitler in his bunker before his death. One was a submarine that could lie on the seabed and fire a rocket with a warhead from beneath the sea – a forerunner of Polaris.'

Hibbert was just in time: on 8 May, the Armistice was signed and the Russians had to stay where they were.

For 30AU and T-Force, the signing of the Armistice, calling an end to hostilities on 8 May, did not change very much. They were no longer fighting the Germans but keeping a wary eye on the Russians, and also embroiled – as, in truth, they had been for several months – in Operation Paperclip.

As the Red Army started its inexorable march towards Germany after its victory at Stalingrad in 1943, the Germans realized that many of their scientists were in considerable danger on the Eastern front and would be needed to defend the homeland – so, too, would the many intellectuals who had been made to serve as ordinary soldiers. One Werner Osenberg oversaw their repatriation, and in March 1945 parts of his list of those involved were found by British forces at the University of Bonn, where they had been stuffed in a lavatory. The Allies had already realized that they needed these men to give them an advantage in what was thought would be the next major war – against Russia; they also realized that it was essential that they were kept out of the Russians' hands. And so Occupation Paperclip was born: to capture as many German scientists as possible and put them to work in the West. The task fell primarily to the three groups of T-Force.

Eventually, hundreds of scientists and their families were relocated to the West – chemists, nuclear physicists, engineers, weapons and rocket experts. Little persuasion was needed, partly because many had a chequered past and feared being put on trial for war crimes, and partly because they had no wish to fall into Russian hands. Perhaps the prize catch was Wernher von Braun, the man responsible for Germany's V1 and V2 rocket programmes, which were underpinned by slave labour drawn from Nazi concentration camps; thousands died, and von Braun must have been aware of what was going on. Nevertheless, he was much feted in America and was directly responsible for the Saturn V rockets that put a man on the moon.

Many of the details of Operation Paperclip are still classified – as is much of the information about 30AU and T-Force. We do know that President Truman had decreed that no active Nazis were to be permitted a safe haven in America, but, with a few exceptions, the US Joint Intelligence Objectives

Agency (JIOS) circumvented his decree by rewriting any of their scientists'
Nazi pasts. Perhaps JIOS was right to do so – after all, the West was to win
the race to put a man on the moon and also win the Cold War. It begs the
question: 'Can the end ever justify the means?'

Above: A captured V2
is test-fired. Though
not the war-winning
weapon Hitler dreamed
of, it was the ancestor
of all subsequent
long-range missiles.

Julius and Ethel Rosenberg

As the Cold War threatened to turn hot, spy mania raged in the USA. Julius and Ethel Rosenberg won lasting notoriety when, in 1951, they were sentenced to death for passing key nuclear secrets to the Russians

FACT FILE

BIRTH: Ethel – 25 September 1915, Julius – 12 May 1918

DEATH: 19 June 1953 at Sing-Sing Prison, New York

MISSION: To secure US military secrets for the Russians, which the Rosenbergs passed to their KGB handlers stationed in the Soviet Consulate in New York. Active 1942–1950

INTELLIGENCE TECHNIQUES: Dead letter-drops, codes, ciphers

FATE: Both Rosenbergs were condemned to death for espionage in 1951 and finally executed in the electric chair in Sing-Sing Prison, New York, two years later after six failed appeals for clemency. Both protested their innocence right until the end. They were the first American civilians ever to be executed for spying in peacetime

ON THE FACE of it, there was nothing particularly untoward about Julius and Ethel Rosenberg. Both were working-class Jews, the son and daughter of two immigrant families. Both lived most of their lives in Manhattan's Lower East Side.

Like many of their contemporaries who had lived through the Great Depression and the rise of fascism, they were political radicals – they had met through their membership of the Young Communist League. But, unlike their peers, they would eventually graduate to become fully-fledged Soviet spies.

According to the FBI, Julius, though younger, was the dominant member of the partnership. He was recruited in 1942 by Russian spymaster Semyon Semenov, a KGB officer then attached to the Soviet Consulate in New York. How far Ethel was involved in actual espionage remains uncertain even today. The least that can be said is that she was aware of her husband's activities even if she did not actively participate in them. Nevertheless, when the Rosenbergs were put on trial, the prosecution demanded the death penalty for both of them.

The Rosenbergs' arrest for spying came about at the end of a long investigative chain that, oddly enough, started in Britain rather than the USA. It began there in 1950, when Klaus Fuchs, a German refugee-physicist who had been made head of the physics department of the British nuclear research centre at Harwell after the war, confessed to having leaked important scientific secrets to a Soviet agent while he was working at Los Alamos on the development of the atom bomb.

Above: Julius and Ethel Rosenberg in custody. Unlike other Soviet agents the FBI arrested, some of whom testified for the state in subsequent treason trials, the Rosenbergs steadfastly refused to cooperate with the authorities.

From Fuchs, the trail led across the Atlantic to Harry Gold, a pudgy Philadelphia-based research chemist. Gold had been working for the Soviets since 1935, when he began to pass on industrial secrets he had stolen from the Pennsylvanian Sugar Company, his former employer. When confronted by the FBI he, too, confessed to being a Soviet spy, acting as contact man not only for Fuchs but also for an American soldier-technician stationed at Los Alamos, who had provided him with information about the atom bomb's detonation mechanism.

Gold claimed not to be able to remember the soldier's name, though he thought his wife was called Ruth and that he was a native New Yorker. Though the lead was a slender one, it was strong enough for the FBI to single out David Greenglass, a soldier-machinist at Los Alamos and Julius Rosenberg's brother-in-law, as Gold's most likely contact. When they showed Gold a photograph of Greenglass, he confirmed that it 'resembled' the man he had been instructed to contact.

When Greenglass was brought in for questioning by the FBI, he quickly made a full confession. The net was now closing in fast on the couple, their acquaintances and associates. Joel Barr, a close college friend, disappeared

Below: Max Elichter, whom Julius Rosenberg had attempted to recruit, was one of the most injurious witnesses in the Rosenberg trial, and not just because of his testimony. Julius and Max had been close friends at college so the betrayal was keenly felt.

in Paris on the day the FBI detained Greenglass, leaving most of his personal possessions behind him. Less than a week later, Morton Sobell, also a college acquaintance, fled by air to Mexico City with his family. Alfred Sarant, another friend, managed to elude FBI surveillance and make a car dash across the Mexican border to vanish without trace. Cleveland scientist William Perl, who denied on oath that he had even known Rosenberg, was less fortunate. He was indicted for perjury.

Like Greenglass and Gold, Max Elitcher, another college acquaintance, chose to cooperate with the FBI. He told its investigators that Rosenberg had tried to recruit him as a spy in 1944. He also described a mysterious incident that had taken place four years later when he, along with Sobell, had made a midnight trip to

a deserted waterfront street in New York City so that Sobell might retrieve a 35-mm film can and bring it back to Rosenberg's apartment. It was enough to enable the FBI to apply successfully for a warrant for Sobell's extradition from Mexico.

On 16 August 1950, after spending the day trying to book a passage on a freighter to Europe, Sobell returned to his Mexico City apartment, where he found armed police waiting for him They forced him into a car and drove him the 800 miles to the Mexican border, where he was handed over to the FBI in Laredo, Texas. Subsequently he was indicted to stand trial with the Rosenbergs as co-defendants.

Greenglass was the prosecution's star witness when the Rosenbergs were put on trial on 6 March 1951 in the Southern District federal court of New York, Judge Irving R. Kaufman presiding. Ten days before the trial started, the FBI offered him a further deal in a final effort to make its case against the Rosenbergs even stronger. Its investigators promised Greenglass not to charge Ruth, his wife, with being a member of the Rosenberg spy ring if he would change his story to implicate Ethel Rosenberg as having been just as much a spy as her husband. Greenglass did not hesitate. He was ready to betray his sister as well as his brother-in-law in order to save Ruth. Originally, he had said that he had handed over secret information to Julius on a New

Above: A photo of Julius Rosenberg taken during the formal arrest proceedings. Though he apparently dropped out of Communist activities in 1943, this was merely a cover; he continued to spy for the KGB.

York street corner. Now, he changed his story. The handover, he swore, had taken place in the living-room of the Rosenberg's New York apartment – and Ethel had been present.

Ruth Greenglass confirmed this story when the prosecution called on her to testify. Indeed, she went further than her husband. She said that Rosenberg had approached her first to ask her husband if he would be prepared to supply him with classified information. She also testified that, on a January day in 1945, she had actually witnessed Ethel busily typing up Greenglass' handwritten notes for forwarding to Gold and the Rosenberg's Soviet controller.

It was damming evidence that the Rosenberg's attorneys – the father-and-son team of Emmanual and Alexander Bloch – failed totally to refute. The best they could do was to suggest that Greenglass and his wife held a grudge against the Rosenbergs as the result of the failure of a business venture in which they had all been involved. Certainly, Judge Kaufman reflected the tide of opinion in the courtroom when he pronounced sentence after the jury found the couple guilty of spying for the Soviets.

'The evidence indicated quite clearly that Julius Rosenberg was the prime mover in this conspiracy', Kaufman stated. 'However, let no mistake be made about the role which his wife, Ethel Rosenberg, played in this conspiracy. Instead of deterring him from pursuing his ignoble cause, she encouraged and assisted the cause. She was a mature woman – almost three years older than her husband and almost seven years older than her younger brother. She was a full-fledged partner in this crime.'

Kaufman's words of condemnation continued: 'Indeed the defendants Julius and Ethel Rosenberg placed their devotion to their cause above their own personal safety and were conscious that they were sacrificing their own children, should their misdeeds be detected – all of which did not deter them from pursuing their course. Love for their cause dominated their lives – it was even greater than their love for their children.'

Perhaps provoked by the Rosenberg's stubborn refusal to answer potentially incriminating questions – they constantly invoked the Fifth Amendment to the constitution, which protected their right to silence during their cross-examinations – Judge Kaufman showed not a smidgeon of compassion.

'I consider your crime worse than murder', he stated baldly. 'Plain deliberate contemplated murder is dwarfed in magnitude by comparison with the crime you have committed. In committing the act of murder, the criminal kills only his victim. The immediate family is brought to grief and when justice is meted out the chapter is closed. But in your case, I believe your conduct in putting into the hands of the Russians the A-bomb years before our best scientists predicted Russia would perfect the bomb has already caused, in my opinion, the Communist aggression in Korea, with the resultant casualties exceeding 50,000 and who knows but that millions more of innocent people may pay the price of your treason.'

'Indeed, by your betrayal you undoubtedly have altered the course of history to the disadvantage of our country.'

WERE THEY GUILTY?

FOR DECADES, THE question of whether Julius and Ethel Rosenberg were guilty of the crimes with which they were charged was a matter of continuous debate. Many left-wingers held that they had been framed by the US authorities and condemned for their Communist sympathies rather than for any crime they actually had committed. In 2008, however, came a revelation that seemed to settle the issue once and for all. The then 91-year-old Morton Sobell, the co-defendant in the Rosenbergs' trial, who had been sentenced to 30 years in prison, finally admitted that he and his friend Julius had both been Soviet agents.

What also helped to clinch the case against Julius – if not his wife – was the public disclosure of the contents of the files of the Venona Project, up until then a little-known effort by US counter-intelligence to intercept and decode diplomatic signals traffic between the Soviet Consulate in New York and Moscow. Through Venona, the US authorities learned that, from 1942 onwards, the USA had been the target of a major Soviet espionage offensive involving dozens of professional Soviet intelligence officers and hundreds of Americans, many of whom were members of the American Communist party. The cables the cryptologists managed to decipher identified 349 citizens, immigrants and permanent residents of the United States who had enjoyed covert relations with the two most significant Soviet intelligence agencies – the KGB and GRU. Julius Rosenberg, or 'Liberal' as he was code-named by the Russians, was high amongst that number.

'No one can say that we do not live in a constant state of tension. We have evidence of your treachery all around us every day – for the civilian defence activities throughout the nation are aimed at preparing us for an atom bomb attack. Nor can it be said in mitigation of the offence that the power which set the conspiracy in motion and profited from it was not openly hostile to the United States at the time of the conspiracy. If this was your excuse the error of your ways in setting yourselves above our properly constituted authorities and the decision of those authorities not to share the information with Russia must now be obvious ...'

'In the light of this, I can only conclude that the defendants entered into this most serious conspiracy against their country with full realization of its implications ... The statute of which the defendants at the bar stand convicted is clear. I have previously stated my view that the verdict of guilty was amply justified by the evidence. In the light of the circumstances, I feel that I must pass such sentence upon the principals in this diabolical conspiracy to destroy a God-fearing nation, which will demonstrate with finality that this nation's security must remain inviolate; that traffic in military secrets, whether promoted by slavish devotion to a foreign ideology or by a desire for monetary gains must cease.'

Below: The eminent French philosopher Jean-Paul Sartre was one of a number of people inside and outside the US who believed that the Rosenbergs were innocent.

The death sentence Kaufman handed down caused international as well as national protest, though somewhat paradoxically Rosenberg himself did not seem that surprised by its severity. 'This death sentence is not surprising', he wrote. 'It had to be. There had to be a Rosenberg case because there had to be an intensification of the hysteria in America to make the Korean War acceptable to the American people. There had to be hysteria and a fear sent through America in order to get increased war budgets.'

If the US authorities thought the case was over and done with, they were soon proved to be wrong. For

Above: Sing Sing Prison, New York, where both Rosenbergs were killed by electrocution in the electric chair on 19 June 1953.

two years, while their lawyers battled to save the lives of the Rosenbergs, protest mounted, especially overseas. Jean-Paul Sartre called the trial 'a legal lynching'; other French protesters said it was the American equivalent of the Dreyfus case. Eminent figures – notably Jean Cocteau, Pablo Picasso, Berthold Brecht, Albert Einstein and even Pope Pius XII – added their voices to the chorus. It was to no avail. On 19 June 1953, President Dwight D. Eisenhower turned down the final appeal for clemency. The same day, a last ditch attempt to get a stay of execution upheld by the Supreme Court failed. Shortly after 8pm that evening Julius and then Ethel died in the electric chair. Both protested their innocence to the end.

It was not the end of the story. In 2008, the Rosenbergs' two sons – who, as children had paraded outside the White House carrying placards reading 'Don't Kill My Mummy and Daddy' – finally conceded that their father had indeed been a Soviet spy all along.

The Cambridge Spies

They were the brightest and best, the cream of Cambridge University's intellectual elite. They were also all Soviet spies, who became possibly the most celebrated spy ring of modern times

THE MOST REMARKABLE spies of the entire Cold War period were four larger-than-life Englishmen: Harold 'Kim' Philby, Guy Burgess, Donald Maclean and Anthony Blunt, who had become friends when they were undergraduates at Cambridge University. All betrayed their country to spy for Moscow.

Like many of their contemporaries at universities elsewhere, Cambridge undergraduates in the 1930s were drawn inexorably into left-wing politics. The Great Depression had led to mass unemployment with millions out of a job. Fascism in Italy and Nazism in Germany were on the march. For many young students at Cambridge, this state of affairs was not just worrying. It was ideologically unacceptable to allow it to go unchallenged.

FACT FILE

CREATED: During the 1930s, the four – Guy Burgess, Anthony Blunt, Donald Maclean and Harold 'Kim' Philby – were recruited to spy for the KGB

MISSION: To penetrate the heart of the British political, diplomatic and social establishment, and to supply British and US military, scientific and diplomatic secrets to the KGB

INTELLIGENCE TECHNIQUES: Codes, ciphers, dead letter boxes, other forms of secret communication

FATE: Burgess and Maclean defected to Russia in 1951. Philby defected in 1963 and worked for the KGB until his death in 1988. Blunt was unmasked in 1964 and publicly exposed in 1979

LEGACY: The KGB regarded 'the magnificent four' as the most effective spy ring it ever possessed

Above: Trinity College, Cambridge, where Maclean, Philby and Burgess were all undergraduates. Blunt, already a Cambridge don, was the man who recruited them for the KGB.

Previous page: The so-called Cambridge Four – clockwise from top left, Anthony Blunt, Donald MacLean, Kim Philby and Guy Burgess – were probably the KGB's most effective British spies.

Philby, Burgess, Maclean and Blunt were four of the brightest and best undergraduates of their generation. They resolved to do something about the situation. They believed that the western democracies would prove to be too feeble to stand up to Hitler and Mussolini – indeed, all the evidence pointed to the fact that they were more than willing to appease them. The Soviet Union, on the other hand, looked powerful and willing enough to take on and defeat Fascism. These beliefs made the Cambridge Four, as they were later christened, easy pickings when they were approached by a recruiter from Moscow. Probably starting with Blunt, the four of them agreed to serve the KGB.

Since the late 1920s, the KGB had been looking out for candidates to spy for it – well-connected clever young men from respected universities being considered the most suitable. The Russians assessed the chances of these young men rising to become members of the elite of the British establishment as being high. They were confident that such agents would soon be well-placed enough to start betraying their country's secrets.

As far as the Cambridge Four were concerned, that was exactly what transpired. By the time the Second World War was underway, Maclean was climbing the diplomatic ladder in the Foreign Office, the flamboyant Burgess was an intimate associate of some prominent political figures and Blunt had joined MI5. Kim Philby, however, was the pick of the bunch. After starting the war as a correspondent for the *Times* of London, he soon became the rising star of MI6, the Secret Intelligence Service.

With the war reaching its climax, things got even better as far as the KGB was concerned. Blunt was on the distribution list for information from Ultra, the war's most secret intelligence operation, which meant that he got sight of all decoded Herman radio traffic. Burgess left the BBC to join Maclean as a high-level diplomat.

To crown it off, just before the war ended, Philby was appointed to be the head of MI6's anti-Soviet section. Amazingly, the man now in charge of running British espionage operations against the Russians was a KGB spy. Philby soon proved his worth to his Soviet controllers by thwarting Britain's post-war plan to infiltrate Albania with exiles returning to their home country, now behind the Iron Curtain and under Communist rule. Having assisted in the formulation of the plan, he then warned the Soviets, who immediately alerted the Albanian Communists to the incursions, so that the exiles could be quickly disposed of upon their entry into the country. Some 300 of them died as a result of the betrayal.

Above: KGB headquarters on Lubianka Square, Moscow. The intelligence the Cambridge Four gathered went straight to the desk of its Director and then to Stalin.

Right: KGB cadet frontier guards on parade. MacLean was particularly informative when the time came to fix boundaries in post-war Eastern Europe as Germany neared final collapse.

In 1944, Maclean was posted to Washington as First Secretary in the British Embassy, where he provided the KGB with detailed information about US nuclear plans and the development of the atomic bomb. Later, he returned to London before being posted to Egypt and then back to London, where he became acting head of the Foreign Office's American Department.

Paradoxically, it was thanks to the CIA that Maclean was eventually exposed as an agent of the KGB. It passed on details to London of what it had discovered about him as a consequence of its initiation of the Venona Project, the interception and decoding of the secret cable traffic between the Soviet Consulate in New York and Moscow. The date of his final identification is uncertain, but it was somewhere between the middle of 1948 and August 1950. He, however, was not placed under MI5 surveillance until the following April and even then the surveillance was restricted to London. The only other move the authorities made was to limit Maclean's hitherto unrestricted access to confidential Foreign Office documentation.

Maclean was aware that something was wrong, but believed that he had been put under observation because of his indiscreet behaviour in Egypt, where his alcoholism had forced his recall. The same thing had happened to Burgess, who had been sacked as Second Secretary at the British Embassy in Washington because of his constant drunkenness. In his case, his promiscuous homosexuality also contributed to the decision to recall him.

Philby, now also stationed in Washington as Chief of Station for MI6, knew better. He told Burgess, who was about to leave the USA for London, to alert Maclean to the danger he was in and, with the help of Yuri Modin, his controller at the Soviet Embassy and Blunt, to extricate Maclean from his precarious situation by arranging his escape from Britain. What Philby did not expect is that Burgess would decide to flee with him. From that time on, Philby referred to Burgess as 'that bloody man'. They never spoke again.

On 25 May 1951, Burgess and Maclean took the midnight ferry from Southampton to St Malo after which they totally disappeared, to resurface a week or so later in Moscow, holed up in an apartment as the guests of the Kremlin. For the next five years, nothing was heard of the pair. British intelligence suspected that they were behind the Iron Curtain, but Soviet officials consistently denied any knowledge of their whereabouts. On 11 February 1956, however, Burgess and Maclean invited a group of Western journalists to a hotel in Moscow, where they gave a brief interview and then handed out a typed joint statement.

In the statement, both men still denied ever having been Soviet spies. However, they formally declared their sympathy with the Soviet Union and stated that they had both been 'increasingly alarmed by the post-war character of Anglo-American policy'. They claimed that their decision to flee Britain was the logical consequence of their belief that only in Russia

WAS THERE A 'FIFTH MAN'?

BURGESS, BLUNT, MACLEAN and Philby were all self-confessed Soviet spies, but controversy still reigns as to whether or not there was also a 'fifth man', who still has not been publicly identified. Over the years, various candidates have been put forward. Chief amongst them was John Cairncross, a British intelligence officer at the time that Burgess and Maclean defected. Oleg Gordievsky, a senior KGB operative who went over to the British in 1984, identified Cairncross as the 'fifth man' in a book he published in 1990.

Other candidates have included Victor Rothschild, Guy Liddell – an MI5 officer who almost rose to become its Director-General before rumours about his possible involvement forced his early retirement in 1953 – and Sir Roger Hollis, Director-General of MI5 for ten years from 1956. Hollis was cleared of any KGB involvement by three separate investigations. Gordievsky himself confirmed their findings, revealing how the KGB itself was baffled by the allegation, attributing it to 'some mysterious, internal British intrigue'.

In 2014, a new candidate emerged. He was Andrew Gow, who had taught at Eton before becoming a Cambridge classics tutor. The eminent art critic Brian Sewell, who had been a close friend and confidant of Blunt, stated that Gow without question had been the mysterious 'fifth man'.

would there be 'some chance of putting into practice in some form the convictions they had always had'. They were certain that the Soviet Union desired a 'mutual understanding' with the West, but that the USA and Britain were adamantly opposed to establishing any such relationship. They concluded by stating, 'Our life in the Soviet Union has convinced us we took at the time the correct decision.'

The spotlight now firmly switched to Philby. In 1951, he had been forced to resign from MI6 following the disappearance of his fellow Cambridge spies. Though Helenus Milmo, the lawyer who led MI5's investigation of Philby, concluded that he found himself 'unable to avoid the conclusion that Philby is and has for many years been a Soviet agent', it was considered that there was insufficient evidence to bring him to trial.

Four years later, MI6 was still staunchly defending its man, even though suspicions about his true loyalties had grown more and more acute in the intervening years. In 1956, he moved to the Lebanon as Middle Eastern correspondent for both *The Observer* and *The Economist*, combining his job as a journalist with part-time work as an agent for MI6. In late 1962, however, he was finally unmasked by Nicholas Elliot, a fellow MI6 officer.

Philby made a confession to Elliot, but he then refused to sign it. The secrecy surrounding the confession was such that Philby continued to be entertained as a guest at the British embassy in Beirut. He was due there for dinner on the night in January 1963 when he disappeared, leaving his wife alone at the party. Though MI6 hoped that Philby might simply have gone into hiding, he, too, had fled to Russia.

This left Blunt as the only one of the Cambridge Four to have escaped detection. His career as an art historian had blossomed. He was appointed Surveyor of the King's Pictures in 1945, was knighted by Queen Elizabeth II in 1956, and became director of the Courtauld Institute of Art and Professor of the History of Art at London University. It looked as if he had avoided discovery completely.

In 1964, however, Michael Straight, an American whom Blunt had recruited for the KGB while he was still a Cambridge don, denounced him to the FBI and MI5 as the long-suspected 'fourth man'. Confronted with Straight's testimony, Blunt confessed to MI5 officer Arthur Martin that April that he had indeed been a Soviet spy. He then made a deal with his interrogators. Blunt agreed that he would hand over, 'all the information I possessed about Russian activities', in exchange for a guarantee that his confession would be kept secret for at least 15 years and that he would be given immunity from prosecution.

MI5 kept its word for more than a decade. Then Blunt made a fatal error. In 1979, he took legal action to prevent the publication of *The Climate of Treason*, a book that contained a thinly-veiled exposure of his treachery. The attempt failed and the press – notably the satirical magazine *Private Eye* – picked up on the story. Ten days after the book's publication, Mrs Thatcher, the recently-elected Conservative Prime Minister, unmasked him as a KGB agent in the House of Commons.

Faced with public disgrace and humiliation, Blunt considered suicide. The Queen stripped him of his title and all his other royal honours. However, he was never hauled into court. He died of a heart attack in 1983, his reputation in tatters and cut off from all but a few remaining friends. In his memoirs, which were eventually published 25 years after his death, he finally conceded that spying for the Soviets had been the biggest mistake of his life.

Below: Kim Philby photographed off-guard hurrying along a Moscow street. After his defection, he continued to work for the KGB for the rest of his life, eventually being awarded the Order of Lenin for his services.

Aldrich Ames

With mounting debts, an alcohol problem, personality defects and a demanding wife, Aldrich Ames was becoming desperate. There seemed to be only one way out: to betray his country for money

FACT FILE

BORN: 26 May 1941, River Falls, Wisconsin

MISSION: To raise money to pay off debts, indulge his character flaws and enjoy an upmarket lifestyle by selling the names of Soviet personnel who were working for the CIA and other foreign intelligence services, as well as details of covert CIA operations and intelligence reports

INTELLIGENCE TECHNIQUES: Use of signal sites to arrange meetings and 'dead drops'; stealing CIA files and computer discs

FATE: Arrested 21 February 1994 and pleaded guilty to spying at his trial in April, following a near eight-year joint CIA/FBI investigation. Now serving a life sentence in a high-security US penitentiary, without the possibility of parole

AFTER A VODKA-FUELLED wait for lunch on 16 April 1985 at the Mayflower Hotel in downtown Washington DC (his guest had stood him up), a bespectacled, dark-haired man sporting a moustache walked down the street, through the door of 1125 Sixteenth Street and handed a note to the receptionist. The building was the Soviet Embassy; the addressee was Stanislas Androsov, a KGB man; the note contained the names of Sergey Motorin and Valery Martynov (both Soviets secretly working for the CIA), a copy of the CIA's internal phone book showing the man's name, and a demand for $50,000. That man was 44-year-old Aldrich Hazen Ames.

Life had started fairly promisingly for Aldrich Ames. He was born in May 1941 in

КПСС!

the small town of River Falls, Wisconsin, one of 2,800 souls according to the 1940 census. His father, Carleton, was a college lecturer who changed careers in 1952 and started working for the CIA as a middle-level analyst. His mother, Rachel (née Aldrich) was an English teacher. Ames – known generally as 'Rick' – enjoyed his time at McLean High School, in MacLean, Virginia, being 'quite witty and friendly' in classmate Corbin Thompson's recollection and a star of the drama society (his mother had been particularly interested in the theatre). But one characteristic was also to the fore: as described later by one of his CIA bosses, 'he exuded this feeling of superiority to everyone else'.

Rick's father Carleton had a difficult time of it in the CIA. After a trip to Burma he was given a negative appraisal because of his heavy drinking. Even so, he managed to wangle Rick a clerical job at the CIA while Rick was at the University of Chicago, starting in 1959. Rick Ames dropped out of university, preoccupied by his interest in the theatre, and later started to work full-time as a clerk at the CIA. By 1969, however, he had completed a history degree at George Washington University and was taken on by the CIA's Career Training Programme.

With hindsight, this was a terrible mistake. Like his father, Rick had started to drink far too much, and there had been a number of incidents involving the police. Again with hindsight, other character flaws had started to become apparent. A paper from Wright University, Ohio, enumerates those of Rick Ames': *alcohol abuse* – many episodes of drunkenness in public, on formal occasion and at work; *grandiosity* – deliberately ignoring CIA rules and regulations on many occasions; *impulsiveness* – a need for excitement and stimulation at the expense of common sense and any feeling of what was appropriate; *self-centredness* – an overbearing arrogance and lack of empathy. All of these flaws were exacerbated by the situations in which he was later to find himself – a divorce; a high-spending new wife; debts; and a fading respect for his employer.

Despite these defects, Ames carved a niche for himself in the CIA – even though, again with hindsight he was lucky to do so. In 1969 he married Nancy Segebarth, another CIA officer, and was posted to Turkey, where his job was to recruit spies. He was not very good at it, succeeding only with a beauty contestant who had a politically ambiguous boyfriend. By 1972, he was back at CIA headquarters. He worked on the Soviet and East European desk with a little more success, but note was being taken of his excessive drinking – at a Christmas party in 1974 he became so drunk

Left: The Turkish capital Ankara was the first location Ames was sent to recruit agents for the CIA. In the three years he spent there, he only recruited one agent, whose utility was questionable.

Above: Rosario Ames is photographed at a wedding reception. Ames had met her through his counter-intelligence activities at the CIA – she had been a CIA informant inside the Colombian Embassy.

that colleagues had to take him home. But in the same year he mastered Russian, and was entrusted with handling a Soviet diplomat called Alexander Dmitrievitch Ogorodnik, code-named 'Trigon,' and he did his job well – even though Trigon eventually killed himself with a cyanide pellet hidden in a pen that Ames had given him.

Ames' superiors were pleased, and gave him a promotion and bonuses. Next, he handled Sergey Fedorenko, a Soviet nuclear weapons expert code-named 'Pyrrhic', before Federenko was called back to Moscow; they had become close friends. Then came Ambassador Arkady Nikolaevich Shevchenko, Under Secretary General at the United Nations.

When it came to handling agents, Ames was flying high, but he still seemed unable to recruit any of them, so he was denied promotion. Disillusioned, and drifting apart from his wife Nancy, he started to get drunk frequently in sleazy bars and hotels and increasingly often ignored the CIA's own security regulations.

In 1981, Ames went under diplomatic cover to Mexico, again to recruit spies; Nancy stayed at home. Again he failed – he was, successful, however, at getting drunk: there are reports of a loud, alcohol-fuelled argument with a Cuban official, and a traffic accident after which he was incapable of answering any questions. Even so, he might have served out his time in the CIA if he had not met Maria del Rosario Casas Depuy, a cultural attaché at the Columbian Embassy to Mexico. They soon started an affair, and when Ames was posted back to America she followed him there. Nancy demanded a divorce, while Rosario, who believed that Ames was much wealthier than he was, ran up unaffordable bills, and in particular huge phone bills to her mother in Bogota.

It was a recipe for disaster – and especially so for an individual with all the character flaws that Ames possessed. By March 1985, Ames had to pay his debts – by now around $34,000 – and come up with a $16,000 divorce settlement for Nancy. To him the only way out seemed to be to sell secrets to the Soviets.

A few days after Ames had received his first $50,000 from the Soviets, given to him by Sergey Chuvakhin, whom he had been trying to meet for some time and had originally stood him up for lunch, he became worried. John

Walker Jr, a retired US Navy man, was arrested and charged with espionage. Ames thought that someone in the embassy who was working for the CIA might have tipped them off, and that he might be next. The answer, he decided, was to do what he called a 'big dump'. That meant that he handed Chuvakhin a list of all the CIA assets that he knew about that were ostensibly working for the Soviets but actually working for the CIA; for good measure, he also gave Chuvakhin a bagful of CIA intelligence reports.

The Soviets, of course, were delighted. They rounded up all those on Ames' list, interrogated them and executed many of them. (One on the

THE MONEY TRAIL

THE CIA ESTIMATES THAT between April 1985 and his arrest in February 1994, Ames was paid some $2.5 million by the Soviets – other estimates have the figure as high as $4.8 million. But what did he and Rosario do with all this money? And how come nobody noticed for so long?

Ames' initial $50,000 payment had soon been spent, on his divorce payment and on settling his debts. But as he was about to leave his posting in Rome, the Soviets promised to pay him $300,000 a year to carry on spying for them – he received most of this by instalments, handed over each time he had lunch with Chuvakhin. Extraordinarily, Ames often deposited them in his bank account on the way home after his lunch. The impression he gave to anybody who took an interest – and not many did – was that all the money came from Rosario's family in Columbia.

In 1989, a CIA accountant called Dan Payne joined a team run by counterintelligence expert Jeanne Vertefeuille. He was given a tip-off by Sandy Grimes, another member of the team, who, in turn, had received it from a family friend of the Ames' called Diana Worthen – a CIA officer herself – she knew that Rosario's family was not wealthy, and saw that the Ames were spending a great deal of money.

Payne started trawling through the Ames bank accounts. He found much to alarm the mole-hunting team: in Rome, Ames had bought a Rolex watch, a Jaguar car, had his teeth capped and exchanged his Ivy League wardrobe for expensive, custom-made silk suits and hand-made shoes. On his return to America, he bought a smart house in Arlington, Virginia for $540,000 in cash and spent $99,000 refurbishing it (Worthen had become suspicious after hearing that new curtains were to be installed throughout); a new Jaguar XJ-6 cost him $50,000 and he spent $6,000 a month on Rosario's phone calls to her family in Columbia. In addition, Rosario spent between $18,000 and £30,000 each month on credit cards at stores such as Neiman Marcus and Nordstrom – after her arrest, FBI agents found dozens of designer dresses and several hundred pairs of shoes. At the time, Ames' CIA salary was $69,843 a year.

How was all this missed? It hardly helped that Vertefeuille's team asked a CIA officer based in Bogota to investigate the finances of Rosario's family. He reported, falsely, that they were, indeed, rich – after asking just their family priest. But eventually Sandra Grimes lost patience. She told Paul Redmond: 'It doesn't take a rocket scientist to figure out what is going on here. Rick is a goddamn Soviet spy.'

And so he was.

list was Colonel Oleg Gordiesvky, the KGB's resident agent in London, who had been spying for Britain's MI6; he was extracted from Russia before he could be arrested, and transported to Britain, where he still lives.) A few months later, Ames also betrayed Sergey Fedorenko, with whom he had become 'good friends'. But for Ames, life was on the up once more: he and Rosario were posted to Rome – and they took a considerable amount of money with them. Ames earned more from the Soviets while in Rome, and then returned to America in 1989; he continued to meet Chuvakhin openly – his story was that he was trying to recruit him – selling more secrets and receiving more money on each occasion.

The sudden loss of their Soviet network caused considerable concern in the corridors of the CIA. A dedicated mole-hunting team was set up, with its leading members being Paul Redmond, Jeanne Vertefeuille and Sandra Grimes. After a number of false leads, some of which were inspired by the Soviets, they started to look at the money trail left behind by their colleagues. Aldrich Ames' name quickly came to the top of the pile.

Below: William J. Casey was head of the CIA from 1981-1987. He oversaw a rapid growth in the intelligence community as the Cold War heated up. It was during his tenure that Ames first began receiving payments from the Soviets.

Now it was over to the FBI, who had the job of arresting spies in America. They bugged his home and car and followed him everywhere. They discovered the mailbox on which he would draw a chalk mark to say that he wanted a meeting; they borrowed his trash can overnight and found an incriminating note in it that referred to a meeting and 'dead drop' sites as well as a printer ribbon that revealed details of letters written to the Soviets. They also found a computer that had auto-saved everything that Ames had written – he had forgotten to turn the feature off. And on the tape of their conversations, they heard Rosario constantly demand more money from Ames and belittle him. The FBI agents were glad to arrest them both on 21 February 1994. After pleading guilty,

Above: Soviet artillery outside a Leningrad barracks building. On the ground, Soviet strength was far greater than that of the NATO forces they would face if the USSR had decided to take the offensive in Europe.

Ames is serving life without the possibility of parole. After a plea bargain, Rosario served a five-year sentence fror conspiracy to commit espionage and tax evasion and was deported back to Columbia upon her release.

For many, Ames' motive was a mystery. Was he driven by a high-minded philosophy, or was it just greed? Ames was to answer the question himself. The author Peter Early managed to interview Ames in prison – until the CIA and FBI found out what was going on and stopped him – where he recorded this revealing quote, recounted in his book *Confessions of a Spy: The Real Story of Aldrich Ames*, published in 1997:

'I would love to say that I did what I did out of some outrage over our country's acts of imperialism or a political statement or out of anger towards the CIA, or even a love of the Soviet Union. But the sad truth is that I did what I did because of the money and I can't get away from that. I wanted a future. I wanted what I saw [Rosario and I] could have together. Taking the money was essential to the recreation of myself and the continuous [sic] of us as a couple.'

And so, as far as he was concerned, his country and his friends could go hang.

The Bay of Pigs

On 17 April 1961, 1,400 Cuban exiles launched an attempted invasion of their homeland at the Bay of Pigs on the southern coast of Cuba. Despite the confidence of the CIA, the invasion was a total flop

KENNEDY WAS AS much to blame as anyone else for the Bay of Pigs fiasco. Before his election to the presidency, he had relentlessly hounded the Eisenhower administration for 'permitting a Communist menace to arise only 90 miles from the shores of the United States.' Now, as President, he had to decide whether or not to allow a CIA-backed armed invasion of the island to go ahead.

Painfully inexperienced in foreign affairs as he was, Kennedy allowed himself to be guided by the experts – men like the veteran CIA Director Allen Dulles, who had won their spurs long ago on the Cold War battlefield. They assured him that the invasion would be swift, sure and – above all – successful. After all, they assured him, Eisenhower himself had approved the basic plan.

FACT FILE

DATE: 17–19 April 1961, Bay of Pigs, south coast of Cuba

MISSION: To overthrow Fidel Castro and his Marxist regime and install a new pro-American government on the island; in 1959 Castro had ousted Fulgericio Batista, a right-wing ally of the USA

INTELLIGENCE TECHNIQUES: Guerrilla infiltration, supply drops

FATE: The invasion was a disaster. Castro was alerted to its coming by poor security among the Cuban exiles, his own intelligence agents and the Soviet KGB. British Intelligence also warned the CIA that the majority of Cubans were firmly behind their leader and there was no chance of a popular insurrection taking place. The CIA had counted on this to support the invaders

Right: President John F. Kennedy was persuaded by the CIA and other senior advisers that Cuba was ripe for a counter-revolution and that the Bay of Pigs landing would meet with little resistance.

Previous page: From the moment Fidel Castro took power in February 1959, he and his Marxist-Leninist regime were on a collision course with the USA.

The reality turned out to be somewhat different. Just four days after the Cuban exiles went ashore. McGeorge Bundy, Kennedy's National Security Advisor, gave him a status report on the progress of the incursion. 'The Cuban armed forces are stronger, the popular response weaker and our tactical position weaker than we had hoped', Bundy told the bewildered President. It was the understatement of the entire disastrous episode. At 2pm the same afternoon, after two days of being pounded by Castro's army and militia, his heavy artillery and tanks, and the Cuban air force, Jose 'Pepe' San Roman, commander of the grandiloquently codenamed Brigade 2506, surrendered. 'Everything is lost', Dulles admitted shamefacedly to former Vice-President Richard M. Nixon. 'The Cuban invasion is a total failure.'

Nikita Khrushchev, the Soviet leader, shared Dulles' view. The fiasco, he believed, was a sure sign of Kennedy's weakness and inexperience – an opinion that was confirmed when he met the President for the first time at the Vienna Summit in April 1962. Within six months of the Summit, Khrushchev was shipping intercontinental ballistic missiles to be installed in Cuba. The world was as close as it ever came to nuclear war.

Above: : Allen Dulles, the long-standing Director of the CIA, persuaded President Kennedy to authorize the Bay of Pigs landings.

It had all looked so different back in March 1960 when President Eisenhower approved the CIA's proposal for a Cuban invasion. The first step was to start recruiting among the thousands of anti-Castro exiles who had taken refuge in the USA. Jose Miro Cardona, a former member of Castro's government, was their leader. As head of the Cuban Revolutionary Council, he was primed to take over as provisional President of the country should the invasion succeed.

CIA-organized camps were established in Guatemala to train the exiles who had been selected to undertake the incursion. By November 1960, a small army of them had been readied to make the initial landing. They would then launch a guerrilla campaign with the aim of bringing down the Castro regime. The plan called for three bombing strikes to be launched against Cuban air bases to destroy Castro's air force on the ground as a preliminary to the launching of the main attack. Paratroops were also to be dropped in advance of the landings to disrupt any attempt made by Cuban ground troops to concentrate to repel the invaders.

Above: Fidel Castro (left) and Ernesto Che Guevara (centre) lead a memorial march in Havana in 1960 for victims of a freight ship explosion. The Kennedy administration feared that Marxist-Leninist principles would spread to South and Central American countries.

The 1,400-strong invasion force would disembark under the cover of darkness to take the defenders by surprise. It would then advance across the island to Matanzas and establish strong defensive positions there. This would be the signal for United Revolutionary Front leaders to fly in from southern Florida and proclaim a provisional government. No US armed forces would be involved openly in any part of the operation.

That at least was the theory, but parts of the plan soon started to unravel when it came to executing it in reality. Almost from the start, lax security among the exiles in Miami and southern Florida, where thousands of Cuban refugees had settled, compromised the operation. As early as November 1960, Cuban military intelligence alerted Castro to the existence of the Guatemalan training camps. Then, the press got in on the act. Kennedy was forced to deny claims that the USA was preparing to support a planned military intervention.

The choice of where to land proved problematic as well. Kennedy and the State Department vetoed the original suggestion of landing at Trinidad, a port with first-rate facilities close to the foothills of the Escambray

Mountains and within striking distance of Havana. It was also a known centre of anti-Castro activities. Instead, the exiles would be put ashore on three beaches on the Bay of Pigs, east of the Zapata peninsula. This was slightly nearer to the Cuban capital than Trinidad, and it was thought that the exiles would find it easier to establish a bridgehead there. However, it was an unfortunate decision. The ground was swampy and difficult to cross, so there was a limited risk that the invading Cubans would get bogged down close to their landing-points.

Then there was the question of air support, which everyone had agreed would be vital. Kennedy vetoed any suggestion that carrier-borne US jets should provide air cover for the invaders. This left the CIA with the 16 obsolete B-26 light bombers that had been made available to it. The idea was to repaint them in Cuban air force colors and recognition markings, and then to fly them from an airstrip in Nicaragua to blitz Castro's airfields. The cover story would be that they were being flown by disaffected members of the Cuban air force, who had defected with their pirated planes to the exiles.

Left: Langley, Virginia, which has been the CIA's headquarters since the 1950s.

The immediate problem was a logistical one. It was a 1,000-mile flight from Nicaragua to the Bay of Pigs and back. This allowed the B-26s to spend less than 40 minutes over their targets. Anything longer and their pilots risked running out of fuel on the return flight somewhere over the Caribbean.

The CIA decided nevertheless to go ahead with the bombing. Then, on 14 April 1961, just three days before the invasion was due to be launched, Kennedy intervened again. He telephoned Richard M. Bissell Jr, the CIA's Deputy Director of Plans and the chief architect of the entire operation. The President asked how many planes Bissell planned to commit. He was told that the CIA would fly all 16 of them. 'Well I don't want it on that scale', Kennedy replied. 'I want it minimal.' Bissell agreed to cut back the number of B-26s by half to just eight. They would strike at the Cuban airfields the next day. It was a drastic diminution of already inadequate air cover – and it was made at Kennedy's insistence. The day before the invasion, he ordered the follow-up air strikes planned by the CIA to be cancelled as well.

Shortly after midnight on 17 April, the 1,400-strong Cuban exile force began to land as planned on the southern coast of its homeland. At dawn, the exiles came under attack from Castro's surviving planes. These quickly sank two of the force's supply ships and drove the others away from shore.

Jose 'Pepe' San Roman, the exiles' commander, radioed his CIA handler for help. 'We are under attack by two Sea Fury aircraft and heavy artillery', he shouted. 'Do not see any friendly air cover as you promised. Need jet support immediately.' The request was denied. San Roman curtly replied, 'You, sir, are a son of a bitch.'

The next day, however, Kennedy relented. He authorized six fighter jets from the aircraft carrier *Essex* to provide one hour of air cover for the CIA's B-26s over the Bay of Pigs' beaches. However, the jets and the B-26s failed to make their rendezvous – the Pentagon had forgotten to allow for the one-hour difference in time zones between the B-26s' base in Nicaragua and the beaches. By this time, Cuban regulars plus their supporting tanks and heavy artillery had joined in what was fast proving to be an unequal battle. The exiles began to run out of ammunition and tactical options. With no direct help forthcoming from the nearby US warships, they were forced back into the swamps around the Bay of Pigs. After they had been flushed out by Castro's triumphant forces – he had arrived on the scene to take direct charge of repelling the invaders – the exiles had no alternative left but to surrender. In Cuba, Castro was hailed by his people as the David who had trounced Goliath.

Some 114 of the exiles had been killed and 1,189 captured. Only a few managed to make it back to the beaches and be evacuated. The prisoners

THE SCAPEGOATS

AFTER THE BAY of Pigs fiasco, the hunt was on for scapegoats. Kennedy ordered the setting up of an immediate inquiry to investigate how the invasion had been planned and executed and establish the reasons for its failure. It was headed by General Maxwell D. Taylor with Attorney-General Robert Kennedy, the President's brother, Admiral Arleigh Burke and CIA Director-General Allan Dulles as its other members.

Taylor pulled few punches in his report. He blamed over-optimism in the CIA for fostering the belief that the invasion would be a walk-over. No attempt whatsoever, for instance, was made to plan an exit strategy for the invaders in the event of a forced withdrawal. Taylor also concluded that the inability to eliminate the Cuban air force was the prime reason for the invasion's failure on the ground. What he did not say openly was that Kennedy himself was much to blame. Determined to try to keep US involvement secret, he refused to authorize direct American military support for the exiles even when the invasion looked like failing. This gave Castro's airmen the chance to sink or drive off the invaders' support ships, which meant that they were cut off from their supplies and then left stranded in their ever-shrinking bridgeheads as the invasion collapsed.

Right: Castro at the United Nations General Assembly. His success in repelling the Bay of Pigs incursion served to substantially strengthen his popularity at home and boost his international prestige.

were transferred to prisons around the island. Some were interrogated live on Cuban television by Castro himself. He told them that he did not intend to have them executed. Instead, he would swap them for tractors and bulldozers. Negotiations with the US government went on sporadically for the next 20 months. Finally, on 24 December 1964, Castro announced that he was releasing the prisoners in exchange for $53 million worth of medical supplies and food. 'As a Christmas bonus', he added, he would allow 1,000 of the prisoners' relatives to accompany them back to the USA.

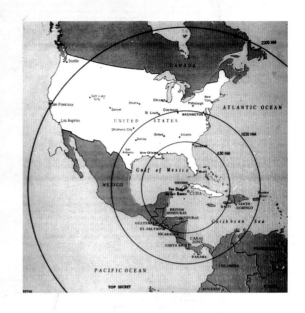

Above: This map shows how far the long-range nuclear missiles the Soviet leader Nikita Khrushchev was preparing to base in Cuba could reach into North and Central America if they were allowed to become operational.

For Kennedy, the fiasco was a humiliation he could not forget. Some sources close to him briefed the media that the President wanted to 'splinter the CIA into a thousand pieces and scatter it to the winds'. For a brief period, he toyed with the notion of direct military intervention and ordered the Joint Chiefs of Staff to draw up a plan for a second invasion of the island to be carried out by the Americans themselves. He soon thought better of the idea. Instead, he opted for Operation Mongoose, a covert attempt to 'provoke, harass or disrupt' the Castro regime. It included a CIA-inspired plan to assassinate the Cuban leader himself. According to J. Edgar Hoover, head of the FBI, Robert Kennedy told him that the CIA was prepared to offer the Mafia '$150,000 to hire some gunmen to go into Cuba and to kill Castro'.

Though Operation Mongoose, too, was eventually abandoned, one Kennedy-sanctioned reprisal against the Cubans has never been lifted. The US embargo on trade with Cuba still remains in place even today.

Operation Wrath of God

In 1972, tragedy struck the Munich Olympics when Palestinian terrorists killed two Israeli athletes and took nine more innocents hostage. Mossad, Israel's equivalent of the CIA, was ordered to exact revenge

FACT FILE

DATE: Authorized by Israeli Prime Minister Golda Meir in 1972; thought to have lasted to at least 1996

MISSION: To track down and eliminate members of the Palestine Liberation Organization and Black September who were thought to have helped to plan, organize and commit the Munich massacre of Israeli athletes, coaches and officials at the 1972 Olympic Games

INTELLIGENCE TECHNIQUES: Letter and telephone bombs, booby-trapped cars and other covert assassination methods

LEGACY: Possibly the most successful manhunt ever, Operation Wrath of God proved to the world that the Israelis would not submit to terrorist violence and would exact retribution for such attacks

FOLLOWING THE MUNICH massacre, Jews everywhere howled for vengeance, especially after the Germans released the three Black September militants who had survived the incident less than two months after the attack occurred. Without consulting the Israelis, Willy Brandt, the West German Chancellor, ordered them to be freed after another group of Black September activists hijacked a Lufthansa plane flying from Damascus to Frankfurt and threatened to kill its passengers and crew unless the Germans gave in to their demands. Brandt later tried to explain away his decision. 'The passengers and crew were threatened with annihilation', he said. 'I then saw no alternative but to yield to this ultimatum and avoid further senseless bloodshed.'

Golda Meir, the tough-minded Prime Minister of Israel, was ready and willing to take action. She authorized two separate operations to exact retribution on those held responsible for the crime. Meir believed that what was planned would have a salutary deterrent effect. The reprisals that she was prepared to sanction would make the Palestine Liberation Organization (PLO), Al Fatah, Black September and other terrorist groups think twice about attacking Israel and Israelis in the future.

Above: Tough-minded Israeli premier Gold Meir, determined to exact vengeance on the planners and perpetrators of the Munich massacre, authorized Mossad to launch Operation Wrath of God in autumn 1972.

Open reprisals started with the launch of Operation Spring of Youth in spring 1973. Carried out by Sayeret Matkal, the Israeli SAS, and led by Ehud Barak, later to be Prime Minister of Israel, who disguised himself as a woman, it took place on 9 and 10 April 9 and targeted individual PLO members in Beirut, the Lebanese capital. Earlier, the Israeli air force had already struck at what were claimed to be terrorist training camps scattered through southern Lebanon and northern Jordan. The bombings resulted in the deaths of anywhere up to 100 PLO members.

Muhammad Yousef (Abu Yousef) al-Najjar, the chief of Al Fatah's military operations in occupied Palestine, was the first to be killed in the Beirut operation. He was asleep when the front door of his apartment was blown out by an explosive charge after which one of Barak's assassination squads burst into his bedroom. His wife, who was also killed, threw herself over her husband's body in a vain attempt to protect him.

Right: Moshe Dayan, Israeli Defence Minister when Operation Wrath of God was activated, unhesitatingly backed the cold-blooded assassination of all the individuals directly or indirectly involved in the Munich attack.

Kamal Adwan, in charge of all Al Fatah's clandestine military operations, was the next to die. When he heard a commotion outside his apartment, he had time to grab hold of a submachine-gun, but he never got the chance to fire it. More Israelis who had broken in through his kitchen window shot him in the head. Kamal Nasser, the head of information for the PLO, was the third and final victim. He tried to fight off his attackers with his pistol, but was speedily shot down as well.

Mossad, the major Israeli intelligence agency, had also already taken up the challenge of exacting a fitting revenge. From the start, Wrath of God was a covert operation, conceived and conducted in utmost secrecy. Its aim was simple – to track down and kill those that the Israelis alleged were directly responsible for the Munich massacre – though many other key Palestinian leaders were killed along the way.

Zvi Zamin, the head of Mossad, who had himself witnessed the shambolic climax of the massacre, chose only his most dedicated agents for the task. One of them, identified only as Yonotan, told *Malariv*, a leading Israeli daily newspaper, decades later in 2006: 'We identified completely with our mission after what the terrorists did to our athletes in Munich. I never asked myself if I was doing the right thing.'

Mike Harari, a veteran Mossad agent, was put in command of the entire operation. Mossad's first target was Wael Zwaiter, a Rome-based Palestinian intellectual. On the evening of 16 October, he was strolling home to his flat in the northern part of the city, reaching his apartment block just after 10:30pm. Two Mossad agents emerged from the shadows and fired 12 bullets into his body at close range. Zwaiter died in the entrance hall.

The second was Dr Mahmoud Hamshari, the PLO's representative in France, who lived in Paris with his French wife Marie-Claude and their young daughter Amina.

In early December 1972, while a Mossad agent posing as an Italian journalist was meeting Hamshari in a café, two explosives experts entered his apartment and planted a bomb under a table by his telephone. The next day, after Marie-Claude had left to take Amina to school, the 'Italian journalist' telephoned Hamshari's home number. 'Is that you, Mr Hamshari?' he asked in Arabic. 'Yes, I am Mahmoud Hamshari,' was the response. The Israelis immediately detonated their bomb by remote control. Hamshari remained conscious for long enough to tell investigating Parisian detectives what had happened. He died later in hospital.

More assassinations in Cyprus, Beirut, Athens, Rome and Paris again, and in Lillehammer, Norway, followed. The 1973 Lillehammer assassination proved to be a huge and costly mistake. Ahmed Bouchiki, a Moroccan waiter with no terrorist associations whatsoever, was gunned down in front of his pregnant wife as they were walking home from a bus stop in the city.

Left: Ali Hassan Salameh (indicated here by arrow) eluded the dogged pursuit of Mossad agents for almost a decade.

A Mossad assassination squad had mistaken him for Ali Hassan Salameh, a close friend of Yasser Arafat, the PLO leader, whom the Israelis suspected of being the brains behind the Munich attack. The mistake came about because of Bouchiki's extraordinarily close physical resemblance to the terrorist the assassination squad had been ordered to hunt down and kill. Unaware it had killed the wrong man, the assassination team prepared to make good its escape. However, the Norwegian police managed to track it down and detain its members as they attempted to board a plane at a nearby airport. Six Israelis were arrested, all of whom were put on trial for their alleged part in the attack. One of them was acquitted, but the other five received prison sentences ranging in severity from two to five and half years. The Norwegian authorities paroled all of them within 22 months.

Mossad was not to be deterred by the Norwegian debacle. If anything, it increased its determination to track down Salameh and eliminate him. The hunt took Mossad agents to Switzerland and then to London. It was there, so it appears, that the enemy struck back.

Above: Five of the victims of the Munich massacre are buried at the Kiryat Shaul Cemetery, Tel Aviv. From left to right, they are André Spitzer, Mark Slavin, Eliezer Halfin, Kehat Shorr and Amitzur Schapira.

One night, a member of the Mossad assassination team met a woman in the bar of his hotel. After a brief conversation, he excused himself and headed back to his room. On the way, he passed his partner in the hallway walking down to the bar for a drink. Shortly afterwards, he returned to the bar to find that both his partner and the woman had disappeared. In time, he returned to his room, which shared a common hallway with the room of his compatriot. He noticed that the room smelled of the same perfume worn by the woman in the bar, and he heard the sound of a woman laughing in his partner's room, He thought no more about it until the following morning, when his partner failed to meet him for breakfast. He went back up to the room and knocked on the door. There was no answer, so he let himself in. There, on the floor, was his partner, shot dead with a gaping bullet wound in his chest.

Remarkably, Mossad managed to locate the woman three months later, living just outside Amsterdam. Covert inquiries into her true identity revealed that she was a freelance assassin, working for anyone who could

THE MUNICH MASSACRE

SHORTLY AFTER 4 AM on 5 September 1972, eight heavily-armed Black September militants scaled a perimeter fence protecting thousands of athletes asleep in Munich's Olympic village. Carrying assault rifles and grenades, the Palestinians ran towards No 31 Connollystrasse, the building housing the Israeli athletes and coaches attending the Olympic Games. Bursting into one apartment, they took six Israeli officials and trainers hostage; in another, they captured the Israeli wrestlers and weightlifters Eliezer Halfin, Yossef Romano, Mark Slavin, David Berger (an Israeli-American law graduate) and Zeev Friedman. When the Israelis tried to fight back, the Palestinians opened fire, killing two of them on the spot. The others were held as hostages. In return for freeing them, the Palestinians demanded the release of 234 of their comrades held in Israeli jails.

After a day of missed deadlines, the Palestinians tired of negotiations. During the evening, their leader demanded a plane to fly his men and the Israelis to the Middle East. German officials agreed to fly the group in two helicopters to an air base on the outskirts of Munich, where a passenger jet would be waiting to fly them to Cairo. Secretly, the Germans began planning a rescue operation at the airfield.

The rescue was botched from start to finish. As soon as they arrived, the Palestinians realized they had walked into a trap. A sporadic gun fight followed, which lasted roughly an hour before German armoured cars, which had got stuck in traffic, belatedly rumbled onto the airfield. On their arrival, the Palestinians panicked. One of them shot the four hostages in one of the helicopters, while another tossed a hand-grenade into the machine. A third terrorist then shot the Israelis in the other helicopter. By the time the German police took control of the situation, all of the hostages and five of the Palestinians were dead.

afford her services. On 21 August, Mossad agents avenged their partner's death by shooting and killing her near her home. It was never learned exactly who had contracted her to kill a Mossad agent.

A fourth attempt to track down Ali Hassan Salameh also failed. This time, he was supposed to be concealed in a house in Tarifa, a small town on the Costa de la Luz on the southernmost part of the Atlantic coast of Spain. Then, in January 1979, Mossad finally struck lucky; at last it had caught up with its elusive quarry.

A female Mossad agent, a 31-year-old British geographer known as Erika Chambers, worked for a charity supporting Palestinian refugees. Once Mossad had established Salameh's likely whereabouts, she travelled to the Middle East and arranged a meeting with him in Beirut, where he was being harboured by the Lebanese government. Having positively identified him, she and the rest of the assassination squad moved in for the kill.

On 22 January, Salameh was travelling down the Rue de Verdun in a convoy of two station wagons, heading to his mother's home for a birthday party. Chambers was painting the scene on the balcony of her apartment, with her red Volkswagen parked in the street below. As Salameh's convoy passed the Volkswagen, a car bomb planted in it by a fellow Mossad agent was exploded by remote control – possibly by Chambers herself.

The blast left Salameh conscious, but severely wounded. He was rushed to hospital, where he died on the operating table. His four bodyguards were also killed in the explosion together with four bystanders, while at least 16 others were injured in the blast. Chambers and her fellow Mossad agents successfully made good their escape.

It was Mossad's great moment, matched only by its alleged assassinations of Mohammed Safady and Adnan Al-Gashey, two of the three surviving Black September militants who had perpetrated the Munich massacre. Jamal Al-Gashey, the sole remaining gunman, is thought to be still alive, living in hiding either in North Africa or Syria. He claims, so it is alleged, still to fear Israeli retribution.

Left: This strikingly modernistic memorial to the 11 Israeli athletes and officials murdered in Munich by Black September operatives during the 1972 Olympic Games stands in the grounds of the Orde Wingate Institute, north of Tel Aviv.

The Canadian Caper

When Iranian students stormed the US Embassy in Tehran in November 1979, six Consular officials escaped capture. The Canadian Embassy hid them for three months until they finally could be smuggled out of the country

FACT FILE

DATE: 6 November 1979 – 27 January 1980

MISSION: To shelter, then help six US diplomats to escape after the storming of the US Embassy in Tehran. The 'Canadian Caper' was organized by the Canadian government with the help of the CIA

INTELLIGENCE TECHNIQUES: Disguise, forged papers and fake identities. They posed as a Hollywood film-crew looking for locations to shoot a science fiction movie as they made their getaway to safety

LEGACY: Ken Taylor, the Canadian Ambassador in Tehran, was hailed as a hero in Canada and the USA. In March 1980, President Ronald Reagan presented him with a Congressional Gold Medal as a tribute to his 'valour, ingenuity and steady nerve'. He was also awarded the Medal of Canada

FEW US PRESIDENTS got it as wrong as Jimmy Carter, when, on New Year's Eve 1977, during a state visit to Iran he confidently opined: 'Iran, because of the great leadership of the Shah, is an island of stability in one of the more troubled areas of the world.' The President spoke way too soon. A week later, the Shah's police shot down dozens of theology students in the holy city of Qom as they demonstrated against a scurrilous attack on the prominent Muslim cleric Ayatollah Khomeini in a pro-government newspaper.

The incident triggered off a year of growing protest that climaxed in a full-blown revolution. The Shah's government collapsed. He was forced out of Iran and into exile.

Above: President Carter prepares to sign a document freezing all official Iranian funds held in US bank accounts; his hope was to persuade the Iranians to release American hostages held at the US Embassy in Tehran.

Previous page: President Jimmy Carter faced his greatest crisis when Iranian revolutionaries stormed the US Embassy in Tehran and took the diplomats there hostage.

US relations with the new regime began to deteriorate speedily. The catalyst was the events that took place on 4 November, when, angered by the US government's decision to allow the exiled Shah into the US for cancer treatment, a mob of young Iranians, mostly radical university students and supporters of Ayatollah Khomeini, laid siege to the US Embassy in Tehran. They surged over the wall around the Embassy compound and broke into its buildings. Most of the embassy personnel in the compound were taken hostage. Their ordeal was to last for the next 14 months.

Six Americans managed to escape capture. Lee Schatz, the Agricultural Attaché, casually strolled through the crowd to take refuge inside the Swedish Embassy. Robert Anders, the head of the Embassy's Consular Section, Joe Stafford, Mark Lijek and the latter's wives also made their way out of the compound unnoticed. Picking their way cautiously through the crowded streets, they were heading initially for the British Embassy when they saw another Iranian mob staging a demonstration directly in their path. Thinking quickly, Anders led the others to his nearby apartment, where they took temporary sanctuary. There they remained, incommunicado for four days until Anders managed to contact John Sheardown, the Canadian Embassy's Chief Immigration Officer. Anders asked if the Canadians would shelter him and his four companions. Sheardown immediately consulted Ken Taylor, the Canadian Ambassador.

Taylor did not hesitate. He was the right man, in the right job, at the right time. He agreed immediately that the Americans must be given shelter, but the question was where? He ruled out the Canadian Embassy itself. Because of its downtown location he considered it insecure and dangerous. Instead, he decided it would be best to split up the group of five. He asked Sheardown to put up three of hostages in his house; he would house the others at his official residence. To keep any curious domestic staff happy, the cover story would be that the guests were simply visiting Canadian tourists.

Above: Ayatollah Khomeini, leader of Iran's Islamic revolution, quickly fell foul of the Americans, who for years had backed the Shah's regime.

Ottawa agreed with Taylor's proposed course of action. The Department of External Affairs cabled him, giving him permission to go ahead and give shelter to the Americans. However, it also warned him that what he was proposing to do must be kept secret at all costs – all knowledge of it was to be on a strict need-to-know basis. The next day, the five Americans were collected and driven to Sheardown's house, where Anders and the Lijeks remained. Taylor took the two Staffords to his ambassadorial residence.

While the Americans waited and fretted, Taylor carried on with his diplomatic duties. He tried hard to get other diplomats to protest with him

about the Iranians' blatant violation of the rules of diplomatic immunity, but met with little success. More crucially, he became the unofficial eyes and ears of Washington in Tehran. He was the go-between the State Department and Bruce Laingen, the US *Chargé d'Affaires*, who was being held in 'protective custody' at the Iranian foreign ministry, which he had been visiting at the time of the attack. He also scouted out possible helicopter landing places in case the US decided to launch a commando-style rescue of the hostages the Iranians were holding.

What happened next took Taylor somewhat by surprise. On 21 November, he took a telephone call from the Swedish Embassy. It was the Swedish Ambassador on the line. He asked him to take over the responsibility of sheltering Lee Schatz, the sixth American escapee, who had been hiding in the apartment of Cecilia Lithander, the Swedish Consul. The Swedes believed he would run less chance of discovery in Canadian hands. Taylor agreed. Schatz joined his colleagues at Sheardown's house, just in time to celebrate Thanksgiving with them.

Over the next weeks, the tension mounted. A lot of it could be put down to sheer boredom. Years later, Mark Lijek summed up the situation. 'We had little to do except read books and play Scrabble', he remembered. 'We drank quite a lot, too.' Even the Canadians' nerves were starting to become frazzled. John Kneale, a First Secretary at the Embassy, recalled how 'we were all in a slew of depression, exhausted and frustrated with no idea how long this paralyzing situation might last'.

More seriously, some of the Canadians feared that the Iranians might realize that not all the Embassy personnel had been accounted for and embark on a manhunt to track down the missing diplomats. The Americans worried that the US might initiate direct military action to liberate the hostages the Iranians were still holding under close guard. If it did – and the operation was successful – the possibility was that the missing diplomats might find themselves left behind in Tehran. If the attempt failed, that would only make their situation worse. There was also the constant risk of accidental discovery by the Iranians to reckon with.

Even more alarmingly, what the Canadians had been doing began to leak out. The inevitable finally occurred in mid-December. Jean Pelletier, the Washington correspondent of the Quebec newspaper *La Presse*, was the man who threatened to break the story. His curiosity was aroused by the fact that the number of Americans being held as hostages by the Iranians

STORMING THE EMBASSY

THE STORMING OF the US Embassy in Tehran was a turning-point in the relationship between the two countries. Years later, Bob Anders, one of the six US diplomats who avoided capture on that fateful day in November 1979, recalled the attack. He remembered every detail as if it was yesterday.

'The embassy compound consisted of 10 or 15 buildings on 27 acres. Our building was up against the back wall of the compound, so when the demonstrators first came in, they broke into the chancery building and tried to get into our building too', Anders told his listeners. He continued: 'We were able to keep them out for a while, but after an hour or so, we heard people up on the roof and somebody said they were trying to start a fire. It was a Marine guard who took a look and saw no one in the street, and told us to make a break for it. There were 30 visitors in the building on business, so we sent them out first, then about 20 Iranian employees next, then finally the 10 Americans in two groups. One group went in one direction and they were captured within a few minutes. Our group managed to get away.'

The hostages taken captive by the Iranians were not as fortunate. They were held in captivity for 444 days until they, too, were eventually released on 20 January 1981.

and the number of Embassy staff did not tally. Told by Gilles Mathieu, the Minister at the Canadian Embassy in Washington, that Canada was 'the most useful ally' the Americans had in the crisis, he concluded that at least some of the American Embassy staff had evaded capture and were being harboured by Canadians. He asked the Embassy to confirm or deny this.

The result was consternation. Ambassador Peter Towe quickly phoned Pelletier, warning him of the risks should the story be broken and urging him to hold off publication. Pelletier, who had already decided that he should keep quiet until the Americans were safely out of Iran, persuaded his editor to agree, but cautioned that other, perhaps less scrupulous, newshounds were on the same trail.

Below: The Shah of Iran and his family pose for photographers after his flight from his country. The US government allowed the exiled Shah to enter the country for medical treatment.

Left: Tony Mendez (centre) poses with freed US diplomats at his Maryland home following the successful conclusion of the 'Canadian Caper'.

Flora MacDonald, the Canadian Minister for External Affairs, was at a NATO meeting in Brussels when she was alerted to the news. She met hastily with US Secretary of State Cyrus Vance and told him that the time had come to get the Americans being sheltered by the Canadians out of Iran. Vance countered by explaining that the hostages held by the Iranians were the Carter administration's priority, but promised to see what could be done when he returned to Washington.

On 30 December, MacDonald and Vance met again at the United Nations in New York. Aware that the *New York Times* was now also aware of what was going on in Tehran – though it, too, had agreed to delay publication – it was clear that the secret could not be kept for much longer. The two decided that Canada and the USA would together devise an urgent rescue plan. In the meantime back in Tehran, Taylor had arranged to rent a safe house, to which the Americans could be moved if the story broke. He counted on having just two to three hours to make the switch before the Iranians would storm his Embassy.

Early in the New Year, the plan got underway, when Tony Mendez, the head of the Authentication Branch of the CIA's Office of Technical

Services, plus a documents specialist, arrived in Ottawa. They were soon closeted with MacDonald and her aides at the minister's apartment. The Canadians issued passports for the six Americans, the idea being to pass them off as Canadian film-makers, working for a dummy film company that Mendez had set up in Hollywood. They were in Iran to explore shooting a possible film production in the country. On Taylor's advice, it was decided that the only safe way out of Iran was through the airport on a scheduled flight.

Meanwhile, the business of closing down the Canadian Embassy had begun. Its staff gradually began to depart, the last classified documents were shredded and unclassified material moved to the New Zealand Embassy, which had agreed to look after Canadian interests. Important information on security procedures at the airport was provided by couriers and departing members of the Embassy staff, including Kneale, who carefully observed and memorized 'every detail of the process' as he passed through the airport on 9 January. Forged Iranian exit and entry visas and passport stamps were prepared in the USA and sent by Canadian courier to Tehran. Luckily, at the last minute, Roger Lucy, the Embassy's Political Officer who was fluent in Farsi, noticed that the entry visas had been wrongly dated.

On 21 January MacDonald ordered the evacuation – or 'exfiltration' as it was termed in bureaucratic jargon – to begin. There was one last delay. The CIA insisted on having its own escort officer on hand. Four days later, Mendez and another CIA officer arrived in Tehran, posing as yet more members of the fictitious film company. One of their tasks was to correct the erroneous date on the entry visas.

The six, plus their CIA escorts, were booked onboard a Swissair flight for Frankfurt, leaving Tehran at 7:35am, on 27 January. It was a Sunday and the airport was relatively quiet. They passed through airport security and passport control with no difficulty. The flight was an hour late taking off, but otherwise there were no hitches. Taylor and the rest of the Embassy staff followed them out of Tehran later the same day.

Back in Washington, Vance requested that the 'strictest confidentiality' about the daring escape should still be preserved. This proved impossible. Pelletier and *La Presse*, broke the story on 29 January – telling the world that after two-and-a-half months in hiding in Tehran, the six Americans were finally home free.

Opposite: The actual hostages did not escape so quickly or so easily. After one botched attempt at rescue, they were eventually freed through diplomatic negotiation on 20 January 1981 – the day of President Ronald Reagan's inauguration. Here they arrive safely on American soil.

Operation Neptune's Spear

After the 11 September 2001 attack on the World Trade Centre in New York, the hunt for Osama bin Laden, leader of al-Qaeda and the world's most wanted man, reached new levels of intensity

FACT FILE

DATE: 2 May 2011

MISSION: To take Osama bin Laden by surprise and capture or kill him before he could escape. US Navy SEALS would fly from Afghanistan in two Black Hawk stealth helicopters and strike at their target – the al-Qaeda leader's compound in Bilal Town, Abbottabad, northwest Pakistan

INTELLIGENCE TECHNIQUES: Covert observation on the ground and by aerial drone, use of informants, spyware and tracking devices on targeted computers and cell phone networks

FATE: Bin Laden and four others were killed. His corpse was recovered and flown to a US aircraft carrier in the Indian Ocean. Once DNA testing had confirmed his identity, the body was disposed of at sea

FOR ALMOST TEN years, bin Laden evaded capture. He was a shadowy figure, from time to time issuing taped *fatwas* on the radio or pre-recorded videos on television. Otherwise, it seems as though he devoted his time to recruiting fanatical Jihadists to join his cause, and to plotting and planning new al-Qaeda attacks. The Americans, who had bungled various opportunities they had had to catch him since the 1990s, were baffled. No one, it appeared, could track bin Laden down and discover his secret hiding place. The suspicion was that, after he had slipped

Right: The Twin Towers blaze as al-Qaeda operatives deliberately fly two hijacked civilian airliners into them on 11 September 2001.

Previous page: Osama bin Laden, founder of al-Qaeda, was responsible for some of the most brutal and destructive terrorist attacks of all time.

through American fingers when he managed to escape capture in the Tora Bora mountain cave complex in Afghanistan, he had taken refuge somewhere across the border in Pakistan, but nobody – least of all Pakistani Intelligence – was sure.

Four months after President Barack Obama had entered the White House, Leon Panetta, the Director-General of the CIA, briefed him on the agency's latest efforts to track down bin Laden. The new President was notably unimpressed. He told Panetta to devise a 'detailed operational plan' to find the Al-Qaeda leader and redouble its efforts to capture him. Al-Qaeda soon became aware of the change. A communiqué blamed the 'very grave' situation they found themselves in on spies who had 'spread throughout the land like locusts'. Nevertheless, bin Laden's trail was still cold.

The breakthrough the CIA so desperately needed came in August 2010, when Panetta returned to the White House with better news. CIA analysts believed that they had pinpointed bin Laden's prize courier.

He was a man in his early thirties named Abu Ahmed al-Kuwaiti. Kuwaiti drove a white SUV whose spare-tyre protector was emblazoned with a picture of a white rhinoceros. The CIA began tracking the vehicle.

One day, a satellite captured images of it pulling into a large concrete compound in Abbottabad, a small town in northwest Pakistan. It appeared that Kuwaiti was living there. The CIA then employed aerial surveillance to keep watch on the compound, which consisted of a three-storey main house, a guesthouse and a few outbuildings. They noted that the compound's residents burned their rubbish, rather than putting it out for public collection, and they also ascertained that the compound had neither a phone nor an Internet connection.

Kuwaiti and his brother, who was also resident in the compound, came and went, but another man, living on the third floor, hardly ever left the main house. On the rare occasions he ventured out, he stayed out of sight behind the compound's walls. Some of the analysts speculated that this man might indeed be bin Laden. The CIA gave him the codename Pacer.

Though excited by the news, Obama was not yet prepared to order the military into action. He ordered a feasibility study to explore his various options. The CIA favoured a surprise helicopter-borne raid that could be launched by a crack detachment of US Navy SEALS. Others, notably Robert Gates, the Secretary of Defence, favoured launching B-2 Sprit bombers in a surprise airstrike instead. When it was pointed out that it would take 32 smart bombs, each weighing 2,000lb, to ensure that the buildings would collapse, the prospect of flattening the entire area gave Obama pause. He discarded the B-2 option and directed Vice-Admiral Bill McRaven to start rehearsing the raid.

Two dozen SEALs were ordered to report to a densely forested site

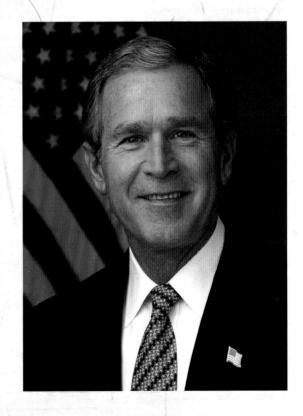

Below: President George W. Bush launched the 'global war on terror' immediately after the Twin Tower attack. He called on bin Laden to be tracked down wherever he was hiding.

in North Carolina for a training exercise on 10 April. There they found a detailed reconstruction of the compound was ready and waiting for them. Five days later, they flew to Nevada for another week of rehearsals.

As the SEALs rehearsed, the assault plan was honed to a smooth finish. The first helicopter was to hover over the yard and drop two ropes, which the 12 SEALs on board would slide down. The second helicopter would fly to the northeast corner of the compound and let four of the SEALs, a Pakistani guide and Cairo, a sniffer dog, disembark. The helicopter would then hover over the house, so that the remaining SEALs could shimmy down to the roof. If bin Laden was proving hard to locate, Cairo would enter the house to sniff him out behind false walls or hidden doors.

On 26 April, the SEAL team left the USA for Bagran airfield, north of Kabul. The next day, Obama gave the raid the official go-ahead. It was to be carried out that Sunday night.

Shortly after 11pm, the Black Hawk helicopters lifted off to embark on their mission, the 26 SEALs safely on board. Some 15 minutes later, they slipped undetected into Pakistani airspace and began their flight to Abbottabad, 120 miles away. The flight time, in total, was 90 minutes.

The Black Hawks approached the town from the northwest, using the mountains on its northern edge for concealment. Then they banked right and flew south along the ridge that marked its eastern perimeter before veering right again towards the centre to make their final approach. Up to this point, all had gone according to plan, but now the pilot of the first Black Hawk ran into difficulties. He aborted the original plan of fast-roping the SEALs into the compound and concentrated simply on getting the machine down safely. He crash-landed astride the security wall in the western part of the compound.

The pilot of the second Black Hawk, unsure whether his colleague had been brought down by ground fire or had suffered mechanical problems, hesitated. Then, he too, abandoned the original plan. Instead of hovering

THE RISE OF AL-QAEDA

BIN LADEN FOUNDED al-Qaeda in 1988. Two years later, it struck for the first time, planting a bomb in a hotel in Aden, Yemen, that had housed American troops on their way to take part in a peacekeeping mission in Somalia. No Americans died in the blast, but two Austrian tourists perished.

Over the next years the organization stepped up its activities. It trained and armed the Somali rebels who killed 18 American servicemen in Mogadishu in 1993. It was also linked to the 1993 bombing of the World Trade Centre, attempted assassination of the then Egyptian president Hosni Mubarak in 1995; the bombing of a US National Guard training centre in Riyadh that same year; and the truck bomb that destroyed the Khobar Towers in Dharan in 1996.

Other outrages swiftly followed. On 7 August 1998, bombs exploded simultaneously at the US Embassies in Nairobi, Kenya, where 213 people were killed and 4,500 injured, and Dar-es-Salaam, Tanzania, where 11 people were killed and 85 injured. Then, on 12 October 2000, a small boat loaded with explosives ploughed into the hull of the Cole, an American destroyer anchored off the coast of Yemen. 17 of the crew were killed and 38 injured. Al-Qaeda took the credit for that incident as well.

A federal grand jury in the USA indicted bin Laden on charges related to the embassy bombings, but, with no defendant present, there could be no trial. Meanwhile, al-Qaeda operatives were busy planning the biggest mission of all – the 11 September attacks on the World Trade Centre and the Pentagon.

Maybe this attack was one step too far even for bin Laden. Though he had proudly vowed that it was al-Qaeda, not the Americans, who would one day, prove to be 'masters of this world', the 'global war on terror' President George W. Bush proclaimed may possibly have surprised him. He was forced into hiding, shifting from place to place and country to country to avoid capture. He was not to emerge from it for the rest of his life.

above the roof of the house as had been intended, he landed in a grassy field across the street.

After a few tense minutes, the SEALs in the first Black Hawk radioed that they were carrying on with the raid. They disembarked hitting the ground running as they made their way alongside the high wall. They reached a metal security gate, which they promptly blew open. They found themselves in an alleyway with their backs to the main entrance to the house. At the end of the alley, they blew their way through another locked gate. They were now in an open courtyard facing the guest-house where bin Laden's courier, al Kuwaiti, and his family were living.

Three Seals broke off to clear the guest-house, shooting al-Kuwaiti and his wife dead. The remaining nine blasted through yet another gate and entered the inner courtyard that faced the main house. Meanwhile, the other SEAL team was also getting into action. Four of its members patrolled the perimeter of the compound, while the others moved inside. They joined up with the SEALs from the first Black Hawk as they were entering the ground floor of the house.

The Seals began making their way through the house, clearing it room by

Below: : A diagram of the Abbottabad compound, where the CIA finally located the world's most wanted man.

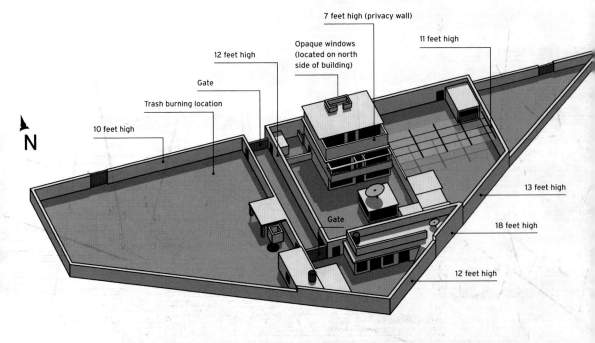

- 7 feet high (privacy wall)
- 11 feet high
- 12 feet high
- Opaque windows (located on north side of building)
- Gate
- Trash burning location
- 10 feet high
- N
- 13 feet high
- Gate
- 18 feet high
- 12 feet high

Left: US Navy SEALs rehearse the rapid insertion techniques they planned to use to access bin Laden's compound before they could be detected and the alarm raised.

room and floor by floor. Three of them blasted their way through a gate that was blocking their progress up the stairs to the first floor. There they met their first resistance. Bin Laden's 23-year-old son, Khalid, opened fire from the top of the stairs. The Seals returned his fire and killed him.

Stepping over Khalid's corpse, the SEALs headed for the second and then the third floor. On the third floor, they found bin Laden himself, hiding unarmed in his bedroom. As the Seals cautiously pushed open the door, two of bin Laden's wives desperately tried to shield his body, while his fifth wife, screaming imprecations in Arabic, attempted to charge them. One of the SEALs brought her down with a shot in her calf. He then grasped the two other women in a bear-hug and forced them away from their husband.

Below: USS Carl Vinson, the aircraft carrier to which bin Laden's body was flown, underway in the Arabian Sea. The Al-Qaeda leader's body was dropped into the sea, to prevent his grave from becoming a shrine for his followers.

Another SEAL trained his M4 carbine on bin Laden. The al-Qaeda chief froze. The SEAL fired two shots, the first one hitting bin Laden squarely in the chest. The second penetrated his head, just below his left eye. Over his radio, the SEAL reported tersely: 'For God and country – Geronimo (the codename for bin Laden), Geronimo, Geronimo!' A second or so later, he added, 'Geronimo EKIA (enemy killed in action).' Back at the White House Situation Room, where Obama and his command

team had been watching and listening to the entire operation, the President said simply 'We got him.'

The SEALS loaded bin Laden's corpse into a body-bag and carried it out to the second Black Hawk. While some SEALs started gathering all the intelligence data they could find, others prepared the damaged Black Hawk for destruction. The rescue Chinook they had summoned now arrived on the scene. As a giant fire started to blaze in the Black Hawk, the SEALs flew off to safety. They had secured the compound and killed bin Laden in just 38 minutes.

The helicopters landed back in Afghanistan at around 3am. Photographs were taken of bin Laden's corpse, and the DNA samples that had been extracted from his bone-marrow were taken away for laboratory examination. At dawn, the al-Qaeda leader began his last journey. His body was flown to the *Carl Vinson*, a US aircraft carrier in the Indian Ocean. Bin Laden's body was washed, wrapped in a white burial shroud, weighted and then slipped inside a burial bag. It was then heaved into the sea. Al-Qaeda was left leaderless.

Above: President Obama and his command team watch in silence in the White House Situation Room as the drama unfolds before them. They tracked the entire operation by video link from an overflying drone.

Index

Acknowledgements

We would like to thank the following for the use of their pictures reproduced in the book:

Alamy, 109, 144, 146, 211
Bundesarchiv, Bild 101 III-Zschaeckel-208-25 / Zschäckel, Friedrich / CC-BY-SA 110
Bundesarchiv, Bild 146III-286 / CC-BY-SA, 145
Bundesarchiv, Bild 183-2004-0330-500 / CC-BY-SA, 147
Corbis, 37, 40, 42, 43, 45, 48, 55, 85, 89, 110, 139, 141, 175, 178, 180, 202, 203, 207, 209, cover
Frontpage, shutterstock.com, 2
Getty, 113, 134, 135, 136, 137, 138, 142, 167, 173, 214
Mary Evans, 106, 109, 111, 117, 154, 157, 195
Muratart, shutterstock.com, 177
RIA Novosti archive, image #129362 / Zelma / CC-BY-SA 3.0, 116
Wikipedia, 11, 12 l/r, 14, 17, 19, 21, 23, 24, 27, 29, 30, 32, 33, 35, 38, 51, 53, 57, 58, 61, 63, 64, 66, 69, 71, 75, 76,
    77, 79, 81, 82, 86, 90, 91, 92, 93, 94, 95, 97, 98, 100, 102, 105, 107, 108, 114, 123, 124, 125, 128, 129, 131, 132, 133,
    151, 152, 153, 159, 160, 161, 162, 164, 165, 168, 169, 170, 176, 180, 183, 184, 185, 186, 187, 188, 190, 191, 193, 194,
    196, 199, 201, 204, 206, 212, 213, 216, 217, 219, back cover

While every effort has been made to credit contributors, the publisher would like to apologise should there
have been any omissions or errors and would be pleased to make the appropriate correction for future
editions of the book.